Everyday Conversation

Published by
Lotus Press Publishers & Distributors

EVERYDAY CONVERSATION

Harsh Sahni

Lotus
PRESS

4735/22, Prakash Deep Building
Ansari Road, Darya Ganj,
New Delhi - 110002

Lotus Press : Publishers & Distributors
Unit No. 220, 2nd Floor, 4735/22, Prakash Deep Building,
Ansari Road, Darya Ganj, New Delhi- 110002
Ph.: 32903912, 23280047, 98188-38000
• E-mail : lotuspress1984@gmail.com
www.lotuspress.co.in

Everyday Conversation

ISBN: 81-8382-191-X

Printed & Published by : **Lotus Press Publisher & Distributors,** New Delhi-02

PREFACE

Language to communicate has made life a lot easier than it would have been millions of years ago. However, as different cultures spread across the world, varying languages developed in different societies that gave each of them not just a way to communicate more fluently, but also a distinct identity.

As time passed and people living far apart explored means of coming closer, they also realised the need to have a language that would bind them socially and help them communicate with each other in a better manner. With this realisation, English language emerged as the best available choice. An interesting aspect of English is that it is a growing language, and has rows of words borrowed from different languages of the world. For this reason, many cultures find it easy to relate with the language, and so can learn it with ease, even if the language falls in the secondary category for them.

The present book on conversation deals with the peculiarities of learning English as a second language and helping the readers grasp it with ease in a manner that they develop good conversation skills. The focus is on helping the readers converse in English fluently and confidently.

Well defined chapters make the reading interesting and the concepts easy to understand. Hope the readers find the book useful enough to help them converse in English easily.

Author

CONTENTS

Adjectives 1

Adjectives describe or give information about nouns or pronouns.

For example:

- The *grey* dog barked. The adjective *grey* describes the noun "dog".)

The good news is that the form of an adjective does not change. It does not matter if the noun being modified is male or female, singular or plural, subject or object.

Some adjectives give us factual information about the noun – age, size colour etc. (fact adjectives – can't be argued with). Some adjectives show what somebody thinks about something or somebody – nice, horrid, beautiful etc. (opinion adjectives – not everyone may agree).

If you are asked questions with which, whose, what kind, or how many, you need an adjective to be able to answer.

There are different types of adjectives in the English language:

- Numeric: six, one hundred and one
- Quantitative: more, all, some, half, more than enough
- Qualitative: colour, size, smell etc.
- Possessive: my, his, their, your
- Interrogative: which, whose, what
- Demonstrative: this, that, those, these

Note: The articles **a, an**, and **the** and the possessives **my, our, your,** and **their** are also adjectives.

Opinion

Adjectives can be used to give your opinion about something.

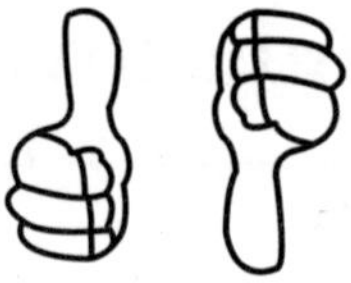

good, pretty, right, wrong, funny, light, happy, sad, full, soft, hard etc.

For example:

- He was a *silly* boy.

Size

Adjectives can be used to describe size.

big, small, little, long, tall, short, same as, etc.

For example:

- "The big man." or "The big woman".

Age

Adjectives can be used to describe ***age***.

For example:

- "He was an *old* man." or "She was an *old* woman."

Shape

Adjectives can be used to describe ***shape***.

round, circular, triangular, rectangular, square, oval, etc.

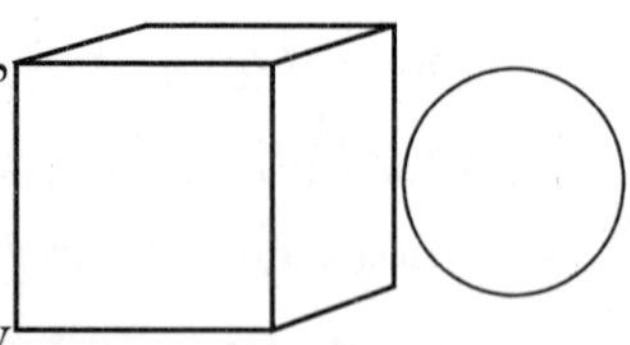

For example:

- "It was a *square* box". or "They were *square* boxes."

Colour

Adjectives can be used to describe colour.

blue, red, green, brown, yellow, black, white, etc.

For example:

- "The blue bag." or "The blue bags".

Origin

Adjectives can be used to describe origin.

For example:

- "It was a *German* flag." or "They were *German* flags."

Material

Adjectives can be used to describe *material*.

- "It was a *cotton* cushion." or "They were *cotton* cushions."

Distance

Adjectives can be used to describe *distance*. Long/Short

long, short, far, around, start, high, low, etc.

For example:

- "She went for a *long* walk." or "She went for lots of *long* walks."

Temperature

Adjectives can be used to describe *temperature*.

cold, warm, hot, cool, etc.

For example:

- "It was a *hot* day." or "Those days were *hot*."

Time

Adjectives can be used to describe *time*.

late, early, bed, nap, dinner, lunch, day, morning, night, etc.

For example:

- "She had an *early* start."

Purpose

Adjectives can be used to describe *purpose. (These adjectives often end with "-ing".)*

For example:

- "She gave them a *sleeping bag.*" or "She gave them *sleeping* bags."

When using more than one adjective to modify a noun, the adjectives may be separated by a conjunction (and) or by commas (,).

For example:

- "Her hair was long and blonde." or "She had long, blonde hair."

More examples:

Adjective	Pretty	Serious	Fast	Quiet
Example	She was a pretty girl.	He was a serious boy.	It was a fast car.	They were quiet children.

Note: Adjectives that go immediately before the noun are called attributive adjectives.

Adjectives can also be used after some verbs. They do not describe the verb, **adverbs** do that. Adjectives after a verb describe the subject of the verb (usually a noun or pronoun). They are called predicative adjectives.

For example:

- "David looks tired." The subject (in this case David) is being described as tired not the verb *to look*.

Comparative Adjectives

When we compare two things or people we look at what makes them different from each other.

For example:

- The camel on the left is taller than the camel on the right.
- A car is faster than a bicycle.

Comparative adjectives are used to show what quality one thing has more or less than the other. They normally come before any other adjectives.

For example:

- The black bag is bigger than the gray bag.

Note: When comparing two things like this we put ***than*** between the adjective and the thing being compared.

For example:

- "Mount Everest is higher ***than*** Mount Snowdon."
- "Arguably, Rome is ***more*** beautiful ***than*** Paris.

Adjective Order

Adjectives can be used to describe opinion, size, age, shape, colour, material, origin and purpose. We can use adjectives together to give a detailed description of something. Adjectives that express opinions usually come before all others.

For example:

- "The big, blue bag."

When we group adjectives together there is a general rule for the position of each type adjective, these are:

Position	**1st**	**2nd**	**3rd**	**4th**	**5th**	**6th**	**7th**	**8th**
	Opinion	**Size**	**Age**	**Shape**	**Colour**	**Material**	**Origin**	**Purpose**
	Nice	Small	Old	Square	Black	Plastic	British	Racing
	Ugly	Big	New	Circular	Blue	Cotton	American	Running

This is just a guide as you wouldn't normally see so many adjectives in one description.

For example:

- "She had a big, ugly, old, baggy, blue, cotton, British, knitting bag" is grammatically correct but a bit too long-winded.
- You might swap opinion and fact adjectives depending on what you wish to emphasise:

For example:

- "She had a long, ugly nose." Emphasising the length of her nose.
- "He was a silly, little man." Emphasising that the man was silly.

Possessive Adjectives

Possessive adjectives are used to show ownership or possession.

Subject pronoun	**Possessive adjective**
i	**my**
you	**your**
he	**his**

she	her
it	its
we	our
they	Their

For example:

- I own this website. = This is *my* website.
- You own this computer (I presume). = It is *your* computer.

Superlative Adjectives

The superlative is used to say what thing or person has the most of a particular quality within a group or of its kind. Superlative adjectives normally come before any other adjectives.

- Mount Snowdon is 3,559 feet high.
- Ben Nevis is 4,408 feet high.
- Snowdon is not the highest mountain in Britain, Ben Nevis is.

Used to something

The use of used to do is explained here. However, **used to** has another meaning, it can be used as an adjective and we use it to talk about things that have become familiar, and are no longer strange or new.

Used to usually comes after verbs such as be, get or become.

- After a while you **get used to** the noise.
- She will **become used to** the smell.
- I **was used to** the web site.

You can also say that someone is used to doing something.

- I'll never get **used to getting** up at six o'clock in the morning.
- It took me a while until I was **used to driving** on the right-hand side of the road.

■

2 Adverbs

Adverbs can tell you where, when, how, why and to what extent something happens.

There are several different classes of adverb.

They are often formed from adjectives or nouns be adding the suffix -ly.

For example:

- Quick becomes quickly, sudden becomes suddenly, intelligent becomes intelligently.

To form an adverb from adjectives ending in *-y* change the *y* to *i* before adding the *-ly*.

For example:

- angry becomes angrily, busy becomes busily,...

To form an adverb from adjectives ending in *-e* drop the *-e* before adding the *-ly*.

For example:

- feeble becomes feebly, true becomes truly,...

Some adjectives ending in -ly need no changes.

For example:

- heavenly,...

However there are exceptions.

For example:

- sly becomes slyly, shy becomes shyly,...

Some adverbs do not end in -ly.

For example: fast, hard, straight,...

Adjective	Pretty	Serious	Fast	Quiet
Example	She was a pretty girl.	He was a serious boy.	It was a fast car.	They were quiet children.
Adverb	Prettily	Seriously	Fast	Quietly
Example	The bird sang prettily.	The policeman spoke seriously.	Schumacher drives fast.	The woman spoke quietly.

Adverbs can modify adjectives

An adjective can be modified by an adverb, which precedes the adjective.

For example:

- That's **really** nice.

Adverbs can modify adverbs

Some adverbs can modify others. As with adjectives, the adverb precedes the one it is modifying.

For example:

- She did it **really well**.

Adverbs can modify nouns

Adverbs can modify nouns to indicate time or place.

For example:

- The concert **tomorrow**.
- The room **upstairs**.

Adverbs can modify noun phrases

Some adverbs of degree such as *quite, rather, so, such...* can modify noun phrases.

For example:

- We had **quite** a good time.
- They're **such** good friends.

Adverbs can modify determiners, numerals and pronouns

Adverbs such as *almost, nearly, hardly, about,* etc., can be used:

For example:

- **Nearly** everyone, who was invited, came to the party.

Adverbs can modify sentences

Some adverbs modify a whole sentence, not just a part of one.

For example:

- ***Luckily** the car stopped in time.* In this sentence *luckily* modifies the whole sentence, it shows that it was good luck that the car stopped in time.

■

Articles 3

First the good news: There are only three articles in English: ***a, an*** and ***the***.

There are two *types* of articles ***indefinite 'a'*** and ***'an'*** or ***definite 'the'***. You also need to know when not to use an article.

The bad news is that their proper use is complex, especially when you get into the advanced use of English. Quite often you have to work it out by what *sounds* right, which can be frustrating for a learner.

Indefinite articles – a and an (determiners)

A and **an** are the indefinite articles. They refer to something not specifically known to the person you are communicating with.

A and **an** are used before nouns that introduce something or someone you have not mentioned before:

For example:

- "I saw ***an*** elephant this morning."
- "I ate ***a*** banana for lunch."
- **A** and **an** are also used when talking about your profession:

For example:

- "I am ***an*** English teacher."
- "I am ***a*** builder."

You use ***a*** when the noun you are referring to begins with a consonant (b, c, d, f, g, h, j, k, l, m, n, p, q, r, s, t, v, w, x, y or z), for example, "**a** city", "**a** factory", and "a hotel".

You use ***an*** when the noun you are referring to begins with a vowel (a, e, i, o, u).

Pronunciation changes this rule. It's the sound that matters, not the spelling.

If the next word begins with a *consonant sound* when we say it, for example, "university" then we use **a**.

If the next word begins with a *vowel sound* when we say it, for example "hour" then we use **an**.

We say "university" with a "y" sound at the beginning as though it were spelt "*you*niversity".

So, "**a** university" IS correct.

We say "hour" with a silent h as though it were spelt "our". So, "**an** hour" IS correct.

(Lots of people get this wrong – including native speakers.)

Definite Article – the (determiners)

Strong pronunciation ð i:

Weak pronunciation ð ə

You use ***the*** when you know that the listener knows or can work out what particular person/thing you are talking about.

For example:

- "**The** apple you ate was rotten."
- "Did you lock **the** car?"
- You should also use ***the*** when you have already mentioned the thing you are talking about.

For example:

- "She's got two children; **a** girl and **a** boy. **The** girl's eight and **the** boy's fourteen."

  We use **the** to talk about geographical points on the globe.

For example:

- **The** North Pole, **the** equator.

  We use **the** to talk about rivers, oceans and seas.

For example:

- **The** Nile, **the** Pacific, **the** English channel.

  We also use **the** before certain nouns when we know there is only one of a particular thing.

For example:

- **The** rain, **the** sun, **the** wind, **the** world, **the** earth, **the** White House etc.

  However if you want to describe a particular instance of these you should use a/an.

For example:

- "I could hear **the** wind." / "There's a cold wind blowing."
- "What are your plans for **the** future?" / "She has **a** promising future ahead of her."

The is also used to say that a particular person or thing being mentioned is the best, most famous, etc. In this use, **'the'** is usually given strong pronunciation:

For example:

- "Harry's Bar is **the** place to go."
- "You don't mean you met **the** Tony Blair, do you?"

For example:

- "**The** books are expensive." = (Not all books are expensive, just the ones I'm talking about.)
- "Books are expensive." = (All books are expensive.)

No article

We usually use no article to talk about things in general:

Inflation is rising.

People are worried about rising crime. (Note! People generally, so no article)

You do not use an article when talking about sports.

For example:

- My son plays **football.**
- **Tennis** is expensive.

You do not use an article before uncountable nouns when talking about them generally.

For example:

- **Information** is important to any organisation.
- **Coffee** is bad for you.

You do not use an article before the names of countries ***except*** where they indicate multiple areas or contain the words (state(s), kingdom, republic, union). Kingdom, state, republic and union are nouns, so they need an article.

For example:

- No article – Italy, Mexico, Bolivia, England.
- Use the – **the** UK (United *Kingdom*), **the** USA (United *States* of America), **the** Irish *Republic.*
- Multiple areas! **the** Netherlands, **the** Philippines, **the** British Isles

■

Case 4

Case is the grammatical function of a noun or pronoun. The three cases in modern English are subjective **(he)**, objective **(him)** and possessive **(his)**.

They may seem more familiar in their old English form – nominative, accusative and genitive. There is no dative case in modern English. First though the good news. You cannot really go wrong here, we have shed most of our cases and as a result English is easier than many other languages because nouns and some indefinite pronouns (*anyone, someone, everyone,* and so on) only have a distinctive case form for the possessive.

However, a remnant of old English is that pronouns have distinctive forms in *all three cases* and must be used with care.

The pronoun cases are simple. There are just three:

1. **Subjective case:** Pronouns used as subject.
2. **Objective case:** Pronouns used as objects of verbs or prepositions.
3. **Possessive case:** Pronouns which express ownership.

Personal Pronoun		
Subjective/ Nominative	**Objective/ Accusative**	**Possessive/ Genitive**
Referring to the subject in a sentence	Referring to the object in a sentence	The apostrophe form of the word ("Lynne's).
I	Me	Mine

You	You	Yours
He	Him	His
She	Her	Hers
It	It	Its
We	Us	Ours
They	Them	Theirs
Who	Whom	Whose

These pronouns, and *who* and its compounds, are the only words that are inflected in all three cases (subjective, objective, possessive). In nouns the first two cases (subjective and objective) are indistinguishable, and are called the common case.

One result of this simplicity is that, the sense of case being almost lost, the few mistakes that can be made are made often, even by native speakers, some of them so often that they are now almost right by prescription.

Objective/Accusative Case

A noun or pronoun is in the objective case when it is used as a direct object, an indirect object, or an object.

A noun which is directly affected by the action of a verb is put into the objective case.

In English we call this noun the "direct object" which is a little more descriptive of its function. It's the direct object of some action.

- Robert fixed *the car*.
- In the example above, the "car" is in the objective case because it's the direct object of Robert's action of fixing.
- Pronouns are inflected to show the objective case.

Personal Pronoun

Objective/Accusative

Referring to the object in a sentence

Me

You

Him

Her

It

Us

Them

Whom

For example:

- The web site gave ***Lynne*** a headache.
- Mum gave ***us*** the money.
- She gave ***him*** the book.

Possessive Case

The good news is that the genetive case is used less and less in English today. Hooray!

You may still hear someone say something like "The mother ***of the*** bride," but it could equally be; "The bride's mother."

However, the possessive pattern ('s) is generally used when indicate a relation of ownership or association with a person, rather than a thing.

For example:

- Lynne's web site kept growing larger and larger.

There are, as ever, exceptions to this rule. When a group of people is involved or animals.

For example:

- The member's forum.
- The dog's tail.

Singular and plural nouns that don't end in 's' take -'s.

For example:

- Lynne's web site.

Plural nouns that end in "s" take an apostrophe (').

For example:

- The girls' dresses.

People's names that end in "s" you can write (') or ('s).

For example:

- Charles' job was on the line.

  or

- Charles's job was on the line.

Pronouns and **determiners** are inflected to show the **possessive case.**

Personal Pronoun/Determiner Possessive	
Lynne's	Lynne's
My	Mine
Your	Yours
His	His
Her	Hers
Its	Its

Our	Ours
Their	Theirs
Whose	Whose

For example:

- This is **Lynne's** web site.
- Have you seen **her** book?
- I think it's **hers**.

Genitive Case

You should still use the genetive case when talking about things that belong to other things.

For example:

- The door **of the** car.
- The content **of the** website.!

Tip – If you aren't sure what to use stick to (of the).

Subjective/Nominative Case

Used especially to identify the subject of a finite verb.

A noun or pronoun is in the subjective when it is used as the subject of the sentence or as a predicate noun. In the following examples, nouns and pronouns in the subjective case are italicized.

A noun in the subjective case is often the subject of a verb.

For example:

- "*The tree* fell on my car", "the tree" is in the nominative case because it's the subject of the verb "fell".

Pronouns are inflected to show the **subjective case**.

Personal Pronoun
Subjective/Nominative

Referring to the subject in a sentence.

I

You

He

She

It

We

They

Who

For example:

- ***Lynne*** owns this web site.
- ***I*** hope to finish my homework tomorrow.
- ***She*** enjoyed her English lessons.
- ***He*** is an *idiot*. (The word idiot is a predicate noun because it follows *is;* a form of the verb "be")

■

Clauses 5

What is a Clause?

A clause is a part of a sentence. There are two main types: independent (main clauses), dependent (subordinate clauses).

Independent Clauses

An independent clause is a complete sentence; it contains a subject and verb and expresses a complete thought in both context and meaning.

For example: The door opened.

Independent clauses can be joined by a co-ordinating conjunction to form complex or compound sentences.

Co-ordinating Conjunctions		
And	**but**	**For**
Or	**nor**	**So**
Yet		

For example: Take two independent clauses and join them together with the conjunction ***and***: "*The door opened.*" "*The man walked in.*" = *The door opened* ***and*** *the man walked in.*

Dependent Clauses

A dependent (subordinate) clause is part of a sentence; it contains a subject and verb but does not express a complete thought. They can make sense on their own, but, they are dependent on the rest of the sentence for context and meaning. They are usually joined to an independent clause to form a complex sentence.

Dependent clauses often begin with a subordinating conjunction or relative pronoun (see below) that makes the clause unable to stand alone.

Subordinating Conjunctions			
After	although	as	because
before	even if	even though	if
in order that	once	provided that	rather than
since	so that	than	that
Though	unless	until	when
Whenever	where	whereas	wherever
Whether	**while**	**why**	

Relative Pronouns		
that	**which**	**Whichever**
who	**whoever**	**Whom**
whose	**whosever**	**Whomever**

For example: The door opened because the man pushed it.

Dependent clauses can be nominal, adverbial or adjectival.

A nominal clause (noun clause) functions like a noun or noun phrase. It is a group of words containing a subject and a finite verb of its own and contains one of the following: ***that* | *if* | *whether.***

For example:

- I wondered **whether** the homework was necessary.

Noun clauses answer questions like "who(m)?" or "what?"

An adverbial clause (adverb clause) is a word or expression in the sentence that functions as an adverb; that is, it tells you something about how the action in the verb was done.

An adverbial clause is separated from the other clauses by any of the following subordinating conjunctions: ***after* | *although* | *as* | *because* | *before* | *if* | *since* | *that* | *though* | *till* | *unless* | *until* | *when* | *where* | *while*.**

For example:

- They will visit you **before** they go to the airport.

Adverbial clauses can also be placed before the main clause without changing the meaning.

For example:

- **Before** they go to the airport, they will visit you.

Adverb clauses answer questions like "when?", "where?", "why?"

An adjectival clause (adjective clause or relative clause) does the work of an adjective and describes a noun, it's usually introduced by a relative pronoun: ***who* | *whom* | *whose* | *that* | *which*.**

For example:

- I went to the show **that** was very popular.

This kind of clause is used to provide extra information about the noun it follows. This can be to define something (a defining clause), or provide unnecessary, but interesting, added information (a non-defining clause).

For example:

- The car **that** is parked in front of the gates will be towed away. (Defining relative clause.)

Information contained in the defining relative clause is

absolutely essential in order for us to be able to identify the car in question.

Information contained in the defining relative clause is absolutely essential in order for us to be able to identify the car in question.

- My dog, **who** is grey and white, chased the postman. (Non-defining relative clause)

A non-defining relative clause is separated from the rest of the sentence by commas. If you take away the non-defining clause the basic meaning of the sentence remains intact.

For example:

- My dog chased the postman.

Adjective clauses answer questions like "which?" or "what kind of?"

Summary

An adjective clause functions as an adjective (modifies a noun or pronoun); an adverb clause functions as an adverb (describes a verb, adjective or other adverb); a noun clause is used as a noun (subject of a verb, direct object, indirect object, predicate nominative or object of the preposition).

Relative Clauses

A relative clause follows the noun it modifies. It is generally indicated by a relative pronoun at the start of the clause, although sometimes you can tell simply by word order. The choice of relative pronoun, or choice to omit one, can be affected by the following:

Human or Non-human?

We make a distinction between an antecedent that is a human — *who(m)* — and an antecedent which is a non-human — *which*.

Who(m) is used when the antecedent is a person.

That is used to refer to either a person or thing.

Which is used to refer to anything except a person.

- I met a man and a woman yesterday. The woman, who had long blonde hair, was very pretty.
- The man she was with, was the man that / who won the race.
- The race was the one that I lost.
- The man, to whom the winnings were given, was with the woman who was very pretty.

Restrictive or Non-restrictive?

Restrictive relative clauses are sometimes called defining relative clauses, or identifying relative clauses.

Similarly, non-restrictive relative clauses are called non-defining or non-identifying relative clauses.

In English a non-restrictive relative clause is preceded by a pause in speech or a comma in writing, unlike a restrictive clause.

For example:

*The builder, **who erects very fine houses**, will make a large profit.* This example, with commas, contains a non-restrictive relative clause.

It refers to a specific builder, and assumes we know which builder is intended. It tells us firstly about his houses, then about his profits.

*The builder **who erects very fine houses** will make a large profit.* This second example uses a restrictive relative clause. Without the commas, the sentence states that any builder who builds such houses will make a profit.

Restrictive		Non-restrictive		
Human	Nonhuman	Human	Nonhuman	
Subject	*who*, *that*	*which*, *that*	*who*	*Which*
Object	*who*, *whom*, *that*, Ø	*which*, *that*, Ø	*who*, *whom*	*Which*
After preposition	*whom*	*which*	*whom*	*Which*
Possessive	*whose*, *of whom*	*whose*, *of which*	*whose*, *of whom*	*whose*, *of which*

■

Conditionals 6

Overview

The conditional tense says that an action is reliant on something else. The two most common conditionals are real and unreal, they are sometimes called if-clauses.

The real conditional (often named 1st Conditional or Conditional Type I) describes situations based on fact.

The unreal conditional (often named 2nd Conditional or Conditional Type II) describes unreal or imaginary situations.

There is also what we call the 3rd conditional (often named Conditional Type III), used to express no possibility of something having happened in the past, and the 0 conditional (often called the zero conditional), used to express absolute certainty.

Unless you are studying English to pass an exam or test don't try to remember the types, just learn the structure so that you know how to express the meaning conveyed by each type.

Note: If the "if" clause comes first, a comma is usually used. If the "if" clause comes second, there is no need for a comma.

1st Conditional/Conditional I

Used to express situations based on fact in the present or future (things which may happen).

Uses the simple present tense:

(IF Clause)	**(Main Clause)**
If I see you tomorrow.	**I will buy you a drink.**

or...

(Main Clause)	**(IF Clause)**
I will buy you a drink.	if I see you tomorrow.

We often use *unless* which means '*if... not*'.

Formation

<table>
<tr><th>(IF Clause)</th><th>(Main Clause)</th></tr>
<tr><td>Unless you hand in your homework,</td><td>I won't mark it.</td></tr>
<tr><td colspan="2">meaning</td></tr>
<tr><td>If you don't hand in your homework,</td><td>I won't mark it.</td></tr>
</table>

or...

<table>
<tr><th>(Main Clause)</th><th>(IF Clause)</th></tr>
<tr><td>I won't mark your homework</td><td>unless you hand it in.</td></tr>
<tr><td colspan="2">means</td></tr>
<tr><td>I won't mark your homework</td><td>if you don't hand it in.</td></tr>
</table>

For example:

- If I have time today, I will phone my friend. = I will phone my friend, if I have time today. (It is possible that I will have time – therefore the condition is real).
- If I go to England, I will buy some Cheddar cheese. = I will buy some Cheddar cheese, if I go to England. (It is possible that I will go to England – therefore the condition is real).

2nd Conditional/Conditional II

Used to express unreal situations in the present or future. Often used to express a wish.

Uses the simple past tense:

Formation

(IF Clause)	(Main Clause)
If I won the lottery,	I would buy a new house.

or...

(Main Clause)	(IF Clause)
I would buy a new house	if I won the lottery.

For example:

- If I were you, I wouldn't do that. = I wouldn't do that, if I were you. (I am not you – therefore the condition is unreal).
- If I had more time, I would do more on my websites. = I would do more on my websites, if I had more time. (I don't have more time – therefore the condition is unreal).

3rd Conditional/Conditional III

Used to express conditions in the past that did not happen. Often used to express criticism or regret with would have, could have or should have.

Uses the past perfect tense:

Formation

(IF Clause)	(Main Clause)
If I had worked harder,	I would have passed my exam.
If I had worked harder,	I could have passed my exam.
If I had worked harder,	I should have passed my exam.

or...

(Main Clause)	(IF Clause)
I would have passed my exam	if I had worked harder.
I could have passed my exam	if I had worked harder.
I should have passed my exam	if I had worked harder.

For example:

- If I hadn't helped you, you would have failed. = You would have failed, if I hadn't helped you. (I helped you so you didn't fail).
- If it had been sunny, we could have gone out. = We could have gone out, if it had been sunny. (We didn't go out because it wasn't sunny).

0 Conditional/Zero Conditional

Used to express general truths and facts (often things based on scientific fact).

Uses the simple present tense:

Formation

(IF Clause)	(Main Clause)
If you heat water to 100°C,	it boils.

or...

(Main Clause)	(IF Clause)
Water boils	if you heat it to 100°C,

For example:

- If you drop an apple, it falls. = An apple falls, if you drop it. (This is an absolute truth based on scientific fact – gravity).
- If you don't do your homework, I will be disappointed. = I will be disappointed, if you don't do your homework. (This is a general truth based on previous knowledge – you know that I am disappointed if people don't do their homework).

■

7 Determiners

Determiners are used in front of nouns to indicate whether you are referring to something specific or something of a particular type.

Determiners are different to pronouns in that a determiner is always followed by a noun. Therefore personal pronouns (*I*, *you*, *he*, etc.) and possessive pronouns (*mine, yours, his,* etc.) cannot be determiners.

The definite and indefinite articles a/an/the are all determiners.

You use a specific determiner when people know exactly which thing(s) or person/people you are talking about.

The specific determiners are:

The definite article: the

Demonstratives: this, that, these, those

Possessives: my, your, his, her, its, our, their

For example:

- "**The** dog barked at **the** boy."
- "**These** apples are rotten."
- "**Their** bus was late."

You use general determiners to talk about people or things without saying exactly who or what they are.

The general determiners are:

The indefinite articles : *a, an*

a few

a little

all

another

any both

each

either

enough

every few

fewer

less

little

many

more

most

much

neither

no

other

several some

For example:

- "**A** man sat under **an** umbrella."
- "Have you got **any** English books that I could have?"
- "There is **enough** food to feed everyone."

Gerunds and Infinitives

Gerunds and infinitives are forms of verbs that act like nouns. They can follow adjectives and other verbs. Gerunds can also follow prepositions.

A gerund (often known as an *-ing* word) is a noun formed from a verb by adding *-ing*. See also Nouns/Gerund. Not all words formed with *-ing* are gerunds.

An infinitive is *to* + the verb.

When a verb follows a verb it either takes the gerund or infinitive form.

Some verbs can take either the gerund or the infinitive with no loss of meaning.

For example:

- With the verb start – "It started *to rain*." or "It started *raining*." Both sentences have the same meaning.

Sometimes the use of the gerund or infinitive changes the meaning of the sentence.

For example:

- With the verb remember – "I remembered *to do* my homework". or "I remembered doing my homework."

In the first sentence (I remembered to do my homework), the person speaking remembered they had some homework first and then carried out the action and did it.

In the second sentence (I remembered doing my homework.), the person speaking carried out the action (their homework) first and then remembered doing it.

Other verbs only take one or the other, unfortunately there is no rule as to which form the verb takes. The same is true when the verb follows an adjective.

Gerunds after Prepositions

When a verb is used after a preposition the verb takes the *-ing* form.

For example:

- You can't make an omelette ***without breaking*** eggs.

■

8 Nouns

A noun is the word that refers to a person, thing or abstract idea. A noun can tell you who or what.

There are several different types of noun:

- There are **common nouns** such as dog, car, chair etc.
- Nouns that refer to things which can be counted (can be singular or plural) are **countable nouns**.
- Nouns that refer to some groups of countable nouns, substances, feelings and types of activity (can only be singular) are **uncountable nouns**.
- Nouns that refer to a group of people or things are **collective nouns**.
- Nouns that refer to people, organisations or places are **proper nouns**, only proper nouns are capitalised.
- Nouns that are made up of two or more words are called **compound nouns**.
- Nouns that are formed from a verb by adding *-ing* are called **gerunds**

Abstract Nouns

An abstract noun is a noun that you cannot sense, it is the name we give to an emotion, ideal or idea. They have no physical existence, you can't see, hear, touch, smell or taste them. The opposite of an abstract noun is a concrete noun.

For example:

Justice; an idea, bravery and happiness are all abstract nouns.

Here is an a-z list of some common abstract nouns:-

adoration	artistry				
belief	bravery				
calm	charity	child-hood	comfort	comp-assion	
dexterity					
ego					
failure	faith	feelings	friend-ship		
happiness	hate	honesty	hope		
idea	impre-ssion	infatu-ation			
joy					
law	liberty	love	loyalty		
maturity	memory				
omen					
peace	pride	principle	power		
redem-ption	romance				
sadness	sensitivity	skill	sleep	success	sympa-thy
talent	thrill	truth			
wit					

Collective/Group Nouns

A collective noun is a noun that is singular in form but refers to a group of people or things.

Sometimes they refer to a group of specific things.

For example:

Tables, chairs, cupboards etc. are grouped under the collective noun ***furniture***.

Plates, saucers, cups and bowls are grouped under the collective noun ***crockery***.

These collective nouns are often uncountable.

Sometimes they are more general.

For example:

Groups of people – Army, audience, band, choir, class, committee, crew, family, gang, jury, orchestra, police, staff, team, trio.

Groups of animals – Colony, flock, herd, pack, pod, school, swarm.

Groups of things – Bunch, bundle, clump, pair, set, stack.

When such a group is considered as a single unit, the collective noun is used with a singular verb and singular pronouns.

For example:

- *The committee has reached its decision*.

But when the focus is on the individual members of the group, British English uses a plural verb and plural pronouns.

For example:

- "*The committee have been arguing all morning*." This is the same as saying "*The people in the committe have been....*"

A determiner in front of a singular collective noun is always singular: *this committee,* never *these committee* (but of course when the collective noun is pluralized, it takes a plural determiner: *these committees*).

Common Nouns

A common noun is a word that names people, places, things, or ideas. They are not the names of a single person, place or thing.

A common noun begins with a lowercase letter unless it is at the beginning of a sentence.

For example:

- People: man, girl, boy, mother, father, child, person, teacher, student.
- Animals: cat, dog, fish, ant, snake.
- Things: book, table, chair, phone.
- Places: school, city, building, shop.
- Ideas: love, hate, idea, pride.

Compound Nouns

A compound noun is a noun that is made up of two or more words. Most compound nouns in English are formed by nouns modified by other nouns or adjectives.

For example:

- The words ***tooth*** and ***paste*** are each nouns in their own right, but if you join them together they form a new word – ***toothpaste***.
- The word ***black*** is an adjective and ***board*** is a noun, but if you join them together they form a new word – ***blackboard***.

In both these examples the first word modifies or describes the second word, telling us what kind of object or person it is, or what its purpose is. And the second part identifies the object or person in question.

Compound nouns can also be formed using the following combinations of words:

Noun	+	Noun	toothpaste
Adjective	+	Noun	monthly ticket
Verb	+	Noun	swimming pool
Preposition	+	Noun	Underground
Noun	+	Verb	Haircut
Noun	+	Preposition	hanger on
Adjective	+	Verb	dry-cleaning
Preposition	+	Verb	Output

The two parts may be written in a number of ways:

1 Sometimes the two words are joined together.

Example: **tooth + paste = toothpaste | bed + room = bedroom.**

2. Sometimes they are joined using a hyphen.

Example: ***check-in.***

3. Sometimes they appear as two separate words.

Example: ***full moon.***

A good dictionary will tell you how you should write each compound noun.

Concrete Nouns

A concrete noun is the name of something or someone that we

experience through our senses, sight, hearing, smell, touch or taste. Most nouns are concrete nouns. The opposite of a concrete noun is an abstract noun.

For example:

- Cats, dogs, tables, chairs, buses, and teachers are all concrete nouns.

Countable Nouns and Uncountable Nouns

A noun can be countable or uncountable. Countable nouns can be "counted", they have a singular and plural form.

For example:

- A book, two books, three books.....
- An apple, two apples, three apples....

Uncountable nouns cannot be counted. This means they have only a singular form. It also means that they do not take a/an before them.

For example:

- Water
- Wine
- Coffee
- Rice

Countable (use a/an or a number in front of countable nouns)	**Uncountable (there is no a/an or number with uncountable nouns)**
An Apple / 1 Apple	Rice
I eat an apple every day.	*I eat rice every day.* (not I eat a rice every day.)

Add (s) to make a countable noun plural	There is no plural form for an uncountable noun
Apples	***rice***
I eat ***an apple*** *every day.* ***Apples are*** *good for health.*	*I eat* ***rice*** *every day.* ***Rice is*** *good for health.*
A computer= *Computers are fun.*	To make uncountable nouns countable add a counting word, such as a unit of measurement, or the general word piece. We use the form "a....... of......."
An elephant=*Elephants are large.*	Rice=*a grain of rice*
	Water=*a glass of water*
	Rain=*a drop of rain*
	Music=*a piece of music*
You can use some and any with countable nouns. *Some dogs can be dangerous.* *I don't use any computers at work.*	**You can use some and any with uncountable nouns.** *I usually drink some wine with my meal.* *I don't usually drink any water with my wine.*

You only use many and few with plural countable nouns. *Many elephants have been hunted.* *There are few elephants in England.*	**You only use much and little with uncountable nouns.** *I don't usually drink much coffee.* *Little wine is undrinkable though.*
You can use a lot of and no with plural countable nouns. *No computers were bought last week.* *A lot of computers were reported broken the week before.*	**You can use a lot of and no with uncountable nouns.** *A lot of wine is drunk in France.* *No wine is drunk in Iran.*

- Sources of confusion with countable and uncountable nouns.
- The notion of countable and uncountable can be confusing. Some supposedly uncountable nouns can behave like countable nouns if we think of them as being in containers, or one of several types.
- This is because 'containers' and 'types' can be counted.
- Believe it or not each of these sentences is correct.
- *Doctors recommend limiting consumption to two* ***coffees*** *a day.* (Here coffees refers to the number of cups of coffee) You could write; "*Doctors recommend limiting consumption to two cups of coffee a day.*"
- *The* ***coffees*** *I prefer are Arabica and Brazilian.*

  (Here coffees refers to different types of coffee)

You could write; "*The types of coffee I prefer are Arabica and Brazilian.*"

Gerund Nouns

A gerund (often known as an -ing word) is a noun formed from a verb by adding *-ing*. It can follow a preposition, adjective and most often another verb.

For example:

- I enjoy *walking*.

■

Participles 9

What is a Participle?

A participle is a word formed from a verb that can function as part of a verb phrase.

For example:

- **has** been

Or independently as an adjective.

For example:

- ***working*** *woman.*

Past Participles.

What is a Past Participle?

A past participle indicates past or completed action or time. It is often called the *'ed'* form as it is formed by adding *d or ed,* to the base form of regular verbs, however it is also formed in various other ways for irregular verbs.

It can be used to form a verb phrase as part of the present perfect tense.

For example:

- I have **learnt** English. (**Learnt** is part of the verb phrase 'have learnt')

  It can be used to form the passive voice.

For example:

- Her hair was well **brushed**.

  It can also be used as an adjective.

For example:

- *As an adjective: He had a* ***broken*** *arm. (****Broken*** *is used here as an adjective.*)

Perfect Participles

What is the Perfect Participle?

The perfect participle indicates completed action. You form the perfect participle by putting the present participle *having* in front of the past participle.

For example:

- having done, having finished, having read, having spoken

  It can be used to form the passive voice.

For example:

- **Having improved** her English Pia's promotion prospects were much better.

Present Participles

What is the Present Participle?

The present participle is a participle that ends in *ing*. It can be used with the auxilliary verb 'to be' to form the continuous tense.

It always takes the 'ing' form of the verb, even irregular verbs have an '...ing' form, in fact virtually all English words that end with 'ing' are present participles.

For example:

- I am **learning** English. (**Learning** is part of the continuous verb phrase 'am learning')
- We were **running** through the woods. (**Running** is part of the continuous verb phrase 'were running').

It can also be used as an adjective.

For example:

- *As an adjective: I am a **working** woman. (**Working** is used here as an adjective.)*

■

10 Pronouns

A pronoun usually refers to something already mentioned in a sentence or piece of text. They are used instead of nouns to prevent repetition of the noun to which they refer. One of the most common pronouns is ***it***.

Example (Singular):

Without a pronoun:

The train was late, **the train** had been delayed. (Sounds horrid, doesn't it?)

With a pronoun:

The train was late, **it** had been delayed. (Much better!)

In this example **the train** is singular, therefore the pronoun must be singular also – **it**.

Example (Plural):

Without a pronoun:

The trains were late, **the trains** had been delayed. (Still sounds horrid, doesn't it?)

With a pronoun:

The trains were late, **they** had been delayed. (Much better!)

In this example **the trains** are plural, therefore the pronoun must be plural also – **they**.

Indefinite Pronoun

Indefinite pronouns refer to things or people without mentioning what or who they are.

For example:

- **Somebody** stole my car.
- Does **anybody** know who she is?

Other indefinite pronouns include – anything, anyone, something, someone, nothing, nobody, none, no one.

Personal Pronouns

Personal Pronoun - Subject	I	you	he/she/it	we	they
Personal Pronoun - Object	me	you	him/her/it	us	them

The personal pronoun is used to refer to someone or something already mentioned (he, she, it etc.), or to refer to the person speaking (I, me etc.) or the person listening (you).

	FORM	**FUNCTION**
First Person Pronoun		
singular	I	subject
	me	object
plural	we	subject
	us	object

Second Person Pronoun		
singular	you	subject
	you	object
plural	you	subject
	you	object
Third Person Pronoun		
singular	he, she, it	subject
	him, her, it	object
plural	they	subject
	them	object

Possessive Pronoun

	I	You (singular and plural)	He/She/It	We	They
Possessive Pronouns	mine	Yours	his/hers/its	ours	Theirs

The possessive pronoun shows who the thing being referred to belongs to or is associated with.

In English these pronouns change form to show their function.

	FORM
First Person Pronoun	
Singular	mine
Plural	ours
Second Person Pronoun	
Singular	yours
Plural	yours
Third Person Pronoun	
Singular	his, hers, its
Plural	theirs

For example:

Q. Whose is this web site?

A. It's mine.

Q. Does Lynne own this web site?

A. Yes, it's hers.

Q. Does Lynne own the Internet?

A. No. It's ours.

Watch out for the following:

Possessive Pronoun	Short Form of 'it is'
its (no apostrophe)	**it's (with apostrophe)**

Reflexive Pronoun

	I	**he/she/it**	**you (singular)**	**you (plural)**	**we**	**They**
Reflexive Pronouns	myself	himself/ herself/itself	yourself	yourselves	ourselves	Themselves

A reflexive pronoun shows that when someone or something affected by an action is the same as the person or thing doing it. This form is used less in English than some other languages.

For example:

- She looked at **herself** in the mirror.
- He washed **himself**.
- They tested **themselves**.

■

Prepositions 11

Prepositions are short words (on, in, to) that usually stand in front of nouns (sometimes also in front of gerund verbs).

Even advanced learners of English find prepositions difficult, as a 1:1 translation is usually not possible. One preposition in your native language might have several translations depending on the situation.

There are hardly any rules as to when to use which preposition. The only way to learn prepositions is looking them up in a **dictionary**, reading a lot in English (**literature**) and learning useful phrases off by heart (**study tips**).

The following table contains rules for some of the most frequently used prepositions in English:

Prepositions – Place (Position and Direction)

English	Usage	Example
on	days of the week	on Monday
in	months/seasons time of day year after a certain period of time *(when?)*	in August/in winter in the morning in 2006 in an hour

at	for *night* for *weekend* a certain point of time *(when?)*	at night at the weekend at half past nine
since	from a certain point of time (past till now)	since 1980
for	over a certain period of time (past till now)	for 2 years
ago	a certain time in the past	2 years ago
before	earlier than a certain point of time	before 2004
to	telling the time	ten to six (5:50)
past	telling the time	ten past six (6:10)
to / till / until	marking the beginning and end of a period of time	from Monday to/ till Friday
till / until	in the sense of *how long something is going to last*	He is on holiday until Friday.
by	in the sense of *at the latest* up to a certain time	I will be back by 6 o'clock. By 11 o'clock, I had read five pages.

Other Important Prepositions

English	Usage	Example
from	who gave it	a present from Jane

of	who/what does it belong to what does it show	a page of the book the picture of a palace
by	who made it	a book by Mark Twain
on	walking or riding on horseback entering a public transport vehicle	on foot, on horseback get on the bus
in	entering a car / Taxi	get in the car
off	leaving a public transport vehicle	get off the train
out of	leaving a car / Taxi	get out of the taxi
by	rise or fall of something travelling (other than walking or horseriding)	prices have risen by 10 percent by car, by bus
at	for *age*	she learned Russian at 45
about	for topics, meaning *what about*	we were talking about you

12 Simple Guide to Asking Questions in English

What is a Question?

A question is a request for information or action.

When writing a question you should always end the sentence with a question mark (?).

Closed Questions

Closed questions demand a yes/no, true/false or right/wrong answer.

When we want to ask **yes/no** questions we can use **do/does, am/is/are** or **have/has** as question words. We use **do** or **have** or **am** with personal pronouns (I), we use **does** or **has** or **is** with third person singular pronouns (he, she, it) and with singular noun forms. We use **do** or **have** or **are** with other personal pronouns (you, we they) and with plural noun forms.

Yes/no questions with the verb **be** are created by moving the verb **be** to the beginning of the sentence. In other words the subject and the verb change their positions in statements and questions.

Statement: I am from England.

Question: Am I from England?

When forming questions in the present continuous tense use the verb be.

I	am	speaking English.	=	Am	I	speaking English?
You	are	speaking English.	=	Are	you	speaking English?
He	is	speaking English.	=	Is	he	speaking English?
She	is	speaking English.	=	Is	she	speaking English?
It	is	speaking English.	=	Is	it	speaking English?
We	are	speaking English.	=	Are	we	speaking English?
They	are	speaking English.	=	Are	they	speaking English?

When forming questions in the present simple tense use the verb **be**, **do**, or **have**. The auxiliary verb is placed before the subject.

To Be

If there is *one verb* in the statement and the verb is a form of *be*, simply switch the positions of the subject and verb.

I	am	English.	=	Am	I	English?
You	are	English.	=	Are	you	English?
He	is	English.	=	Is	he	English?
She	is	English.	=	Is	she	English?
It	is	English.	=	Is	it	English?
We	are	English.	=	Are	we	English?
They	are	English.	=	Are	they	English?

To Do

If there is *one verb* in the statement and the verb is *do*, simply switch the positions of the subject and verb.

I	do.	=	Do	I?
You	do.	=	Do	you?
He	does.	=	Does	he?
She	does.	=	Does	she?
It	does.	=	Does	it?
We	do.	=	Do	we?
They	do.	=	Do	they?

To Have

If there is *one verb* in the statement and the verb is *have*, (with or without got to show possession), switch the positions of the subject and verb.

I	have	(got) an English book.	=	Have	I	(got) an English book?
You	have	(got) an English book	=	Have	you	(got) an English book?
He	has	(got) an English book	=	Has	he	(got) an English book?
She	has	(got) an English book	=	Has	she	(got) an English book?
It	has	(got) an English book	=	Has	it	(got) an English book?
We	have	(got) an English book	=	Have	we	(got) an English book?
They	have	(got) an English book	=	Have	they	(got) an English book?

We can also form this style of question with **Do...have...?** here there is no subject-verb inversion, do is placed before the subject.

I	have breakfast every morning.	=	Do	I	have breakfast every morning?
You	have breakfast every morning.	=	Do	you	have breakfast every morning?
He	**has** breakfast every morning.	=	Does	he	**have** breakfast every morning?
She	**has** breakfast every morning.	=	Does	she	**have** breakfast every morning?
It	**has** breakfast every morning.	=	Does	it	**have** breakfast every morning?
We	have breakfast every morning.	=	Do	we	have breakfast every morning?
They	have breakfast every morning.	=	Do	they	have breakfast every morning?

If there is one verb, and the verb is **not** a form of *be*, the process is more complex. To form a question add the correct form of the verb 'to do' to the beginning. Here there is no subject verb inversion.

I	speak English.	=	Do	I	speak English?
You	speak English.	=	Do	you	speak English?
He	speaks English.	=	Does	he	speak English?

She	speaks English.	=	Does	she	speak English?
It	speaks English.	=	Does	it	speak English?
We	speak English.	=	Do	we	speak English?
They	speak English.	=	Do	they	speak English?

Answering a Closed Question

For example: "Are you from England?"

You can answer closed questions with "Yes" or "No".

You can also answer closed questions with a slightly longer answer "Yes, I am." or "No, I'm not."

Finally you can answer closed questions in the long form "Yes, I am from England." or "No, I'm not from England."

Open Questions

Open questions leave room for a description or opinion, and are more useful in eliciting information.

Open questions are often called Wh.. questions:

There are eight wh-questions - ***what, when, where, which, who, whom, whose*** and ***why*** and to this list we usually add ***how*** as they are all used to elicit particular kinds of information.

You use *what* when you are asking for information about something.

You use *when* to ask about the time that something happened or will happen.

You use *where* to ask questions about place or position.

You use *which* when you are asking for information about one of a limited number of things.

You use *who* or *whom* when you are asking about someone's identity.

You use *whose* to ask about possession.

You use *why* to ask for a reason.

You use *how* to ask about the way in which something is done.

Question word	**Verb**	**+**	**Answer**
What	is	your name?	My name is Lynne.
When	is	the party?	The party is on Tuesday.
Where	are	you from?	I'm from England.
Which	is	your car?	The red car is mine.
Who	are	you?	I'm Lynne.
Whose	is	this web site?	It's mine.
Why	is	this web site here?	Because it is!
How	are	you?	I'm fine thanks.

What, which and **whose** can be used with or without a noun as a question word.

For example:

- What time is it? = What is the time?
- Which car is yours? = Which is your car?
- Whose web site is this? = Whose is this web site?

Whom can only be used to elicit information about the object of the sentence. Although using whom would be grammatically correct, we normally use who instead because it doesn't sound so formal.

For example:

- "Whom did you see?" would normally be expressed as "Who did you see?"

Who, what, which and whose can all be used to elicit information about the subject or object of the sentence.

For example:

- If the answer is "I ate the banana." the object question would be "What did you eat?" and the subject question would be "Who ate the banana?"

Object Questions

Object questions ask about the object of a sentence. The word order of the question must be changed and the question requires the use of the auxiliary verb 'to do'.

For example:

- If the answer is, "I caught the train to London." The question would be, "Which train did you catch?"
- If the answer is, "I saw a film yesterday." The question would be, "What did you do yesterday?"

Subject Questions

There are also subject questions. These are questions that we ask to find out about the subject. When what, which, who or whose refers to the subject, the question word comes before the verb without the use of the auxiliary verb.

For example:

- If the answer is, "The train to London was late." The question would be, "Which train was late?"
- If the answer is, "I won the race." The question would be, "Who won the race?"

More examples:

Object questions:

- What did you do today?
- Which film did you like best?
- Who did I phone?

Subject questions:

- What happened today?
- Which film is best?
- Who phoned me?

Tag Questions

What is a Tag Question?

A tag question is a short question added to the end of a positive or negative statement.

For example:

He is,	isn't he?
He does,	doesn't he?
He will,	won't he?
He can,	can't he?

How are they formed?

Normally a positive statement is followed by a negative tag, and a negative statement is followed by a positive tag.

For example:

+	–
You're English,	**aren't** you?
–	+
You're not German,	**are** you?

The verb in the statement should be the same tense as the verb in the tag.

For example:

Present tense	**Present tense**
You **are** a good singer,	**aren't** you?
Past tense	**Past tense**
You **didn't** go to work yesterday,	**did** you?
Present perfect tense	**Present perfect tense**
You **have been** to London,	**haven't** you?

If the verb used in the statement is an auxiliary verb, then the verb used in the tag must match it. If a modal (can, could, will, should, etc.) is used in the statement, then the same modal is used in the tag part.

If the statement doesn't use an auxilliary verb, then the auxiliary *do* is used in the tag part.

For example:

Auxiliary verb	
She **is** from England,	**isn't** she?
They **aren't** very nice,	**are** they?
She **doesn't like** it here,	**does** she?
Modal verb	
You **can** sing,	**can't** you?
They **shouldn't** do that,	**should** they?
No auxiliary	
He **eats** meat,	**doesn't** he?

Why do we use them?

Tag questions are used to verify or check information that we think is true or to check information that we aren't sure is true. Sometimes we just use them for effect.

We show the meaning of the tag question through intonation.

If the tag is a real question it has a rising intonation.

For example:

- The chairman's coming at 3.00, isn'**t he**?

If the tag is not a real question it has a flat or falling intonation.

For example:

- It's a nice day today, **isn**'t it?

! It is possible for a positive statement to be followed by a positive tag for even more effect (sarcasm, anger, disbelief, shock, concern etc.).

For example:

- *Oh you* **will, will** *you?*
- *You* **think** *you're funny,* **do** *you?*

Direct and Indirect Speech

We often have to give information about what people say or think. In order to do this you can use direct or quoted speech, or indirect or reported speech.

Direct Speech

Saying exactly what someone has said is called direct speech (sometimes called quoted speech)

Here what a person says appears within quotation marks ("...") and should be word for word.

For example:

She said, "Today's lesson is on presentations."

or

"Today's lesson is on presentations," she said.

Indirect Speech

Indirect speech (sometimes called reported speech), doesn't use quotation marks to enclose what the person said and it doesn't have to be word for word.

When reporting speech the tense usually changes. This is because when we use reported speech, we are usually talking about a time in the past (because obviously the person who spoke originally spoke in the past). The verbs therefore usually have to be in the past too.

For example:

Direct speech	Indirect speech
"I'm going to the cinema", he said.	He said he was going to the cinema.

Tense Change

As a rule when you report something someone has said you go back a tense: (the tense on the left changes to the tense on the right):

Direct speech		Indirect speech
Present simple She said, "It's cold."	›	**Past simple** She said it was cold.
Present continuous She said, "I'm teaching English online."	›	**Past continuous** She said she was teaching English online.
Present perfect simple She said, "I've been on the web since 1999."	›	**Past perfect simple** She said she had been on the web since 1999.
Present perfect continuous She said, "I've been teaching English for seven years."	›	**Past perfect continuous** She said she had been teaching English for seven years.
Past simple She said, "I taught online yesterday."	›	**Past perfect** She said she had taught online yesterday.

Past continuous She said, "I was teaching earlier."	›	**Past perfect continuous** She said she had been teaching earlier.
Past perfect She said, "The lesson had already started when he arrived."	›	**Past perfect** NO CHANGE – She said the lesson had already started when he arrived.
Past perfect continuous She said, "I'd already been teaching for five minutes."	›	**Past perfect continuous** NO CHANGE – She said she'd already been teaching for five minutes.

Modal verb forms also sometimes change:

Direct speech		Indirect speech
will She said, "I'll teach English online tomorrow."	›	**would** She said she would teach English online tomorrow.
can She said, "I can teach English online."	›	**could** She said she could teach English online.
must She said, "I must have a computer to teach English online."	›	**had to** She said she had to have a computer to teach English online.

shall She said, "What shall we learn today?"	›	**should** She asked what we should learn today.
may She said, "May I open a new browser?"	›	**might** She asked if she might open a new browser.

Direct speech	Indirect speech
"I might go to the cinema", he said.	He said he might go to the cinema.

You can use the present tense in reported speech if you want to say that something is still true i.e. my name has always been and will always be Lynne so:-

Direct speech	Indirect speech
"My name is Lynne", she said.	*She said her name was Lynne.* *or* *She said her name is Lynne.*

You can also use the present tense if you are talking about a future event.

Direct speech (exact quote)	Indirect speech (not exact)
"Next week's lesson is on reported speech ", she said.	*She said next week's lesson is on reported speech.*

Time Change

If the reported sentence contains an expression of time, you must change it to fit in with the time of reporting. For example we need to change words like *here* and *yesterday* if they have different meanings at the time and place of reporting.

<table>
<tr><th colspan="2">Today</th><th>+ 24 hours – Indirect speech</th></tr>
<tr><td colspan="2">"Today's lesson is on presentations."</td><td>She said yesterday's lesson was on presentations.</td></tr>
<tr><th colspan="3">Expressions of time if reported on a different day</th></tr>
<tr><td>this (evening)</td><td>›</td><td>that (evening)</td></tr>
<tr><td>Today</td><td>›</td><td>yesterday...</td></tr>
<tr><td>these (days)</td><td>›</td><td>those (days)</td></tr>
<tr><td>now</td><td>›</td><td>then</td></tr>
<tr><td>(a week) ago</td><td>›</td><td>(a week) before</td></tr>
<tr><td>last weekend</td><td>›</td><td>the weekend before last / the previous weekend</td></tr>
<tr><td>here</td><td>›</td><td>there</td></tr>
<tr><td>next (week)</td><td>›</td><td>the following (week)</td></tr>
<tr><td>tomorrow</td><td>›</td><td>the next/following day</td></tr>
</table>

In addition if you report something that someone said in a different place to where you heard it you must change the place (here) to the place (there).

For example:

At work	At home
"How long have you worked here?"	She asked me how long I'd worked there.

Pronoun Change

In reported speech, the pronoun often changes.

For example:

Me	*You*
"I teach English online."	***She** said she teaches English online.*

Reporting Verbs

Said, told and *asked* are the most common verbs used in indirect speech.

We use ***asked*** to report questions:

For example: I **asked** Lynne what time the lesson started.

We use ***told*** with an object.

For example: Lynne **told** me she felt tired.

We usually use ***said*** without an object.

*For example: Lynne **said** she was going to teach online.*

If said is used with an object we must include ***to***;

For example: Lynne **said to** me that she'd never been to China.

For example: Lynne **told** me that she'd never been to China.

There are many other verbs we can use apart from said, told and asked.

These include:

accused, admitted, advised, alleged, agreed, apologised, begged, boasted, complained, denied, explained, implied, invited, offered, ordered, promised, replied, suggested and thought.

Using them properly can make what you say much more interesting and informative.

For example:

He asked me to come to the party.

He invited me to the party.

He begged me to come to the party.

He ordered me to come to the party.

He advised me to come to the party.

He suggested I should come to the party.

Use of 'That' in reported speech

In reported speech, the word ***that*** is often used.

For example:

*He told me **that** he lived in Greenwich.*

However, *that* is optional.

For example:

He told me he lived in Greenwich.

For example:

He asked me if I would come to the party.

■

13 Simple Capitalisation Guide

Capitalisation

Capital letters are used for two main purposes in English:

- to show the beginning of a sentence.
- to show that a noun is a proper noun.

1. The first letter of every new sentence is capitalised. *For example:*

   The postman delivered the parcel. **It** was very heavy.

2. The pronoun **I** is always capitalised.

   For example:

   My name is Lynne, **I** am a teacher.

3. Proper nouns (also called proper names) are the words which name specific people, organisations or places. They always start with a capital letter.

For example:

Each part of a person's name is a proper noun:

- Lynne Hand - Elizabeth Helen Ruth Jones...

The names of companies, organisations or trade marks:

- Microsoft - Rolls Royce - the Round Table - WWW

Given or pet names of animals:

- Lassie Trigger Sam

The names of cities and countries and words derived from those proper nouns:

- Paris - London - New York - England - English

Geographical and Celestial Names:

- The Red Sea - Alpha Centauri - Mars

Monuments, buildings, meeting rooms:

- The Taj Mahal - The Eiffel Tower - Room 222

Historical events, documents, laws, and periods:

- The Civil War - The Industrial Revolution - World War I

Months, days of the week, holidays:

- Monday - Christmas - December

Religions, deities, scriptures:

- God - Christ - Jehovah - Christianity - Judaism - Islam - the Bible - The Koran - The Torah
- Ram - Krishna - Durga - Ramayana - Mahabharat - Hinduism - Buddhism - Vedas - Christ - God - Jehovah - Mohammed - Christianity - Islam - Judaism - The Bible - The Koran - The Torah

Awards, vehicles, vehicle models and names, brand names:

- Paramvir Chakra - Arjuna Award - The Bharat Ratna - Dronacharya Award - The Nobel Peace Prize - Ford Focus - The Bismarck - Tata Group - Bharat Petroleum - Sahara India Parivar - Essar Group

■

14 Simple Pluralisation Guide

Plural Noun Forms

Regular Plurals

The plural form of most nouns is created simply by adding the letter '*s*' to the end of the word.

For example:

- minute - minutes

Nouns that end in *-ch, -x, -s, -sh*, z or *s-like* sounds, the plural is formed by adding '*es*' to the end of the word.

For example:

- church - churches | box - boxes | gas - gases | bush - bushes | ass - asses

Nouns that end in a single, the plural is formed by adding '*zes*' to the end of the word.

For example:

- quiz - quizzes

Most nouns ending in *-o* preceded by a consonant also form their plurals by adding '*es*'.

For example:

- potato - potatoes | tomato - tomatoes | volcano - volcanoes

However many newly created words and words with a Spanish or Italian origin that end in *-o* just add an '*s*'.

For example:

- photo - photos | piano - pianos | portico - porticos

Nouns ending in a consonant + *y*, drop the *y* and add '*ies*'.

For example:

- party - parties | lady - ladies

Most nouns ending in *-f* or *-fe*, drop the *f* and add '*ves*'.

For example:

- calf - calves | half - halves | wolf - wolves

Irregular Plurals

There are many common nouns that have irregular plurals.

For example:

- child - children | person - people | foot - feet | mouse - mice | tooth - teeth

Some nouns have identical plural and singular forms, although they are still considered to have a plural form.

For example:

- aircraft - aircraft | fish - fish | headquarters - headquarters | sheep - sheep | species - species

Uncountable nouns on the other hand have no plural form and take a singular verb (is / was...).

For example:

- advice | information | luggage | news

Some nouns (especially those associated with two things) exist only in the plural form and take a plural verb (are / were...).

For example:

- cattle | scissors | trousers | tweezers | congratulations | pyjamas

Nouns that stem from older forms of English or are of foreign origin often have odd plurals.

For example:

- analysis - analyses | crisis - crises | ox - oxen | index - indices or indexes

In **compound nouns** the plural ending is usually added to the main noun.

For example:

- court martial - courts martial | son-in-law - sons-in-law | passer-by - passers-by

■

Simple Guide to Prefixes 15

What is a Prefix?

A prefix (affix) is a word, or letter(s) placed at the beginning of another word (a base word) to adjust or qualify its usage or meaning. The opposite of prefix is suffix.

Prefix	General Meaning	Example
a(n)-	not, without	atonality, asexuality, amoral, anarchy
ab-	away	abduction, absolutism, ablution
ac-		
acr(o)-	high, up	Acropolis
aden(o)-		
aer(o)-	air	aeronautics, aerodrome, aeroplane, aerodynamics
agr(o)-	relating to farming	agriculture
an-		
an(a)-	out of	anachronism
an(o)-		

andr-	man	androgyny, androcentrism, android, androgen
anem-		
Anglo-	English or British	Anglo-Irish relations, anglophile
ante-	before	antebellum
anth-rop(o)-	relating to human beings	anthropology, anthropocentrism, anthropomorphic
ant(i)-	against	antidote, antibody, anticlockwise
aut(o)-	self	autonomy, autobiography, automobile, autopilot
bar(o)-	atmosphere	
bathy-	deep	Bathyscape, Bathysphere
be-	completely, thoroughly; excessively; on; around; about; used to form transitive verbs	
bi-	two	bicycle, bijection, bilingual, bicameralism, bisexuality
bi(o)-	life	biology, biography, biosphere, biotechnology
bibli(o)-	relating to books	bibliophilia, bibliography

blast(o)-		
brady-	slow	bradycardia
brom(o)-		
bronch(o)-	relating to breathing	bronchitis
cac(o)-		
cardi(o)-	heart	cardiovascular
cent-, centi -	hundred or hundredth	centenary, centimeter, centipede
cephal(o)-		
chrom(o)-, chromat(o)-		
chron(o)-	time	chronology, chronograph
circum-	around	circumcision, circumnavigation, circumlocution, circumference
cion(o)-		
co-	together	cooperative, cohabit
colpo-		
com-, con-, col-, cor-	with, together	conference, connotation, context, Congress, congregation
contr(a)-, contr(o)	against, opposite	contradiction, contraception, controversy
cosm(o)-		cosmology, cosmopolitan, cosmotheism

counter-	against, opposite	counterpoint, counterweight, counter-reformation
crin(o)-		
cry(o)-	frost, icy cold	cryogenics, cryoelectronics, cryostorage
crypt(o)-	hidden	cryptography, cryptozoology
cyt(o)-	hollow, receptacle, cell	cytoplasm, cytology
dactyl(o)-		
de-	taking something away, the opposite	decentralisation, deforestation, dehydration
dec(a)-, dek(a)-	ten	decamerous
deci -	one tenth	deciliter
dem(o)-	people, nation	demographics, democracy
derm(o)-, derm(a)-, dermat-	skin	dermatology, dermatitis
di-	two, double	
didact(o)-	apt at teaching	
dynam(o)-	power, force	dynamic, dynamite, dynamo
dis-	reverse, opposite	dissent, discovery, disambiguation
dox(o)-	Doxology	

dys-	bad, deformed, abnormal	dyspepsia, dystrophy, dysarthria
eco-	house	economy, ecology, ecosystem, ecotourism, ecotage
ecto(s)-	outside	ectoskeleton
edaph(o)-		
electr(o)-	electricity	electrocution
embry(o)-	full	
encephal(o)-	brain	encephalitis
end(o)-, ent(o)-		
enne(a)-	nine	enneastyle
enter(o)-		
eo-	dawn, early	eobacterium
ep(i)-, eph-	above	epitaxy
erg(o)-		ergonomics
erythr(o)-		
erot(o)-		
stom(o)-, stomat(o)-		
ethn(o)-		ethnology, ethnolinguistics, ethnocentrism
eu-	good	eulogy, euthanasia, eugenics, euphemism

ex-	former	ex-wife, ex-president
ex(o)-	outside	exoskeleton
extra-	very, more than usual, outside, beyond	extra-thin, extra-special extraordinary, extraterrestrial
flor(i)-	relating to flowers	florist
fore-	before, in advance	foreskin, foreshadowing
gyn-	female	gynaecology, gynoid
hemi-	half	hemimetabolous
hex(a)-	six	hexapod
hyper-	excessive, (least to greatest in order: hypo, sub, super, hyper)	hyperactive, hyperthyroidism
hyp(o)-	below, (least to greatest in order: hypo, sub, super, hyper)	hypodermic
in-	extremely	inflammable, invaluable
in-, il-, im-, ir-	not	infallibility, illiteracy, immoral, irrelevant
inter-	between, from one to another	intervention, international
intra-	within, interior	intramural, intravenous

kilo-	thousand	kilogram, kilowatt
mal-	bad, badly	malpractice, malnutrition
maxi-	most, very, large	maxi-dress
mega-, megal-	million, very large	megabyte, megaphone
meta-	after, beyond	metacarpal, metaphysics
micro-	one millionth, very small	microgram, microorganism, micronation
mid-	in the middle of	mid-term elections, Mid-Autumn Festival, Mid-Atlantic Ridge
milli-	thousandth	milligram, millilitre
mini-	small	miniskirt, miniscule
mis-	bad, wrong	miscarriage, misanthropy, misogyny
mon(o)-	one, single	monolith, monorail, monotony, monocle
multi-	many	multiculturalism, multilingual
non-	not	nonsense, non-denial
non-	nine	none, nonagon
oct(o)-, oct(a)-	eight	octane, octopod, octagon
oo- ("oo - oh")	egg, ovum	oocyte

out-	more, to a greater degree	to outdo, to outrun
over-	more than normal, too much	overpopulation, over-consumption
pent(a)-	five	pentagon
post-	after	Post-Fordism, postpartum depression, postmodernity, postmodernism
pre-	before	prediction, preview, precedent, prenatal care
pro-	for, in favour of	pro-choice, pro-life, promotion
quadr-, quart-	four	quadrangle, quadruplet, quartic, quartile
quin(que)-	five, into five parts	quinquesection
quint(i)-	fifth, five	quintiped
re-	again, repeatedly	reduction, reflection, revolution
rect(i)-	proper, straight	rectify, rectangle
scler(o)-	hard	scleroderma atherosclerosis
semi-	half	semi-automatic, semi-detached
sept(a)-	seven	heptachord
sex(i)-	six	sexivalent
Sino-	Chinese	Sino-American relations

spasm(o)-		
sperm(o)-, spermat(o)-		
spher(o)-		
sphygm(o)-	pulso	sphygmomanometer
splen(o)-		
splanchn(o)-		
schiz(o)-, schist(o)-	split	schizophrenia, schistocyte
staphyl(o)-		
styl(o)-	pillar	
sub-	below, less than, under,(least to greatest in order: hypo, sub, super, hyper)	subset, subsonic, subway, subtitles
super-	extremely, more than, (least to greatest in order: hypo, sub, super, hyper)	superhuman, superego, supersonic
syn-	along with, together, at the same time	synergy, synchronicity
tach(y)-, tach(o)-	fast, speed	tachycardia, tachometer

tel(e)-, tel(o)-	far, over a long distance	telecommunications, television, telephoto lens, telodynamic
tel(o)-, tel(e)-	end, complete, mature	teloblast
trans-	across, beyond	transfer, transubstantiation, transatlantic, Trans-Siberian railway
tri-	three	triangle, tricolour, triptych
ultra-	extremely, beyond a certain limit	Ultramontanism, ultraviolet
un-	not, opposite, take something away	unconstitutional, undelete
uni-	one, single	uniform, unification
ur-	first, original	urtext
zoo- ("zoo -oh")	relating to animals	zoomorphic, zoology

■

Building a Sentence 16

A sentence is a group of words which starts with a capital letter and ends with a full stop (.), question mark (?) or exclamation mark (!). A sentence contains or implies a predicate and a subject.

Sentences contain clauses.

Simple sentences have one clause.

Compound sentences and complex sentences have two or more clauses.

Sentences can contain subjects and objects.

The subject in a sentence is generally the person or thing carrying out an action. The object in a sentence is involved in an action but does not carry it out, the object comes after the verb.

For example:

- The boy climbed a tree.

If you want to say more about the subject (the boy) or the object (the tree), you can add an adjective.

For example:

- The young boy climbed a tall tree.

If you want to say more about how he climbed the tree you can use an adverb.

For example:

The young boy quickly climbed a tall tree.

The sentence becomes more interesting as it gives the reader or listener more information.

There are more things you can add to enrich your sentence.

Parts of a sentence	Description
Adjective	Describes things or people.
Adverb	Alters the meaning of the verb slightly.
Article	a, an – indefinite articles the – definite articles
Conjunction	Joins words or sentences together.
Interjection	A short word showing emotion or feeling.
Noun	Names things
Preposition	Relates one thing to another.
Pronoun	used instead of a noun to avoid repetition.
Proper noun (subject)	The actual names of people or places etc.
Verb	Action or doing word.

What makes a Complete Sentence?

If it helps you, think about a sentence as if it were a skeleton, the skeleton contains various bones and these bones are put together to form different parts of the body. So are sentences formed by words, the words are the bones and they are put together in different ways to form sentences.

Simple Sentences

A simple sentence contains a single subject and predicate. It describes only one thing, idea or question, and has only one verb – it contains only an independent (main) clause.

Any independent clause can stand alone as a sentence. It has a subject and a verb and expresses a complete thought.

For example:

- Jill reads.

Even the addition of adjectives, adverbs, and prepositional phrases to a simple sentence does not change it into a complex sentence.

For example:

- The brown dog with the red collar always barks loudly.

Even if you join several nouns with a conjunction, or several verbs with a conjunction, it remains a simple sentence.

For example:

- The dog barked and growled loudly.

Compound Sentences

Compound sentences are made up of two or more simple sentences combined using a conjunction such as ***and***, ***or*** or ***but***.

They are made up of more than one independent clause joined together with a co-ordinating conjunction.

For example:

"The sun was setting in the west and the moon was just rising."

Each clause can stand alone as a sentence.

For example:

"The sun was setting in the west. The moon was just rising."

Every clause is like a sentence with a subject and a verb. A coordinating conjunction goes in the middle of the sentence, it is the word that joins the two clauses together, the most common are (***and, or, but***)

For example:

- I walked to the shops, ***but*** my husband drove.
- I might watch the film, ***or*** I might visit my friends.
- My friend enjoyed the film, ***but*** she didn't like the actor.

Complex Sentences

Complex sentences describe more than one thing or idea and have more than one verb in them. They are made up of more than one clause, an independent clause (that can stand by itself) and a dependent (subordinate) clause (which cannot stand by itself).

For example:

- "My mother likes dogs that don't bark."
- Dependent clauses can be nominal, adverbial or adjectival.

■

The Verb 17

The verb is the fundamental part of the sentence. The rest of the sentence, with the exception of the subject, depends very much on the verb. It is important to have a good knowledge of the forms used after each verb (verb patterns), for example: to tell [someone] to do [something]

Here we can see that the verb to tell is followed immediately by a person (the indirect object, explained later), an infinitive with 'to', and, possibly, an object for the verb you substitute for DO.

Verbs also show a state of being. Such verbs, called BE VERBS or LINKING VERBS, include words such as: am, is, are, was, were, be, been, being, became, seem, appear, and sometimes verbs of the senses like tastes, feels, looks, hears, and smells.

For example:

- "Beer and wine ***are*** my favourite drinks." The verb "are" is a linking (be) verb.

Fortunately, there are only a limited number of different verb patterns. Verbs can describe the **action** (something the subject actually does) or **state** (something that is true of the subject) of the subject.

For example:

- ACTION: I play football twice a week.
- STATE: I've got a car.

Some verbs can represent both actions and states, depending on the context.

For example ***work:***

- ACTION: David's ***working*** in the bank.
- STATE: David ***works*** in a bank.

Finding the Verb

When you analyse a sentence, first identify the verb. The verb names and asserts the action or state of the sentence.

For example:

- "Working at the computer all day ***made*** David's head ache."

The main verb of the sentence is "***made***", not working.

Verbs identify our activity or state.

For example:

- eat, sleep, run, jump, study, think, digest, shout, walk....

The Subject

The subject is the person or thing the sentence is 'about'. Often (but not always) it will be the first part of the sentence. The subject will usually be a noun phrase (a noun and the words, such as adjectives, that modify it) followed by a verb.

Finding the Subject

Once you determine the verb, ask a *wh...?* question of the verb. This will locate the subject(s).

For example:

- David works hard.
- Who "works hard"? = David does = the subject.
- Beer and wine are my favourite drinks.

- What "are my favourite drinks"? Beer and wine are=the subjects.

The subject(s) of a sentence will answer the questions, "who or what."

The Predicate

Once you have identified the subject, the remainder of the sentence tells us what the subject does or did. This part of the sentence is the predicate of the sentence.

The predicate always includes the verb and the words which come after the verb.

For example:

- Michael Schumaker drove the race car.
- "Michael Schumaker" is the subject; "drove the race car" is the predicate.

More Advanced Terminology

The Object

Some verbs have an object (always a noun or pronoun). The object is the person or thing affected by the action described in the verb.

Objects come in two types, direct and indirect.

The direct object refers to a person or thing affected by the action of the verb.

For example:

- "He opened ***the door***. "- here the door is the direct object as it is the thing being affected by the verb to open.

The indirect object refers to a person or thing who receives the direct object.

For example:

- "I gave ***him*** the book." – here ***him*** *(he)* is the indirect object as he is the beneficiary of the action.

Transitive/Intransitive verbs

Verbs which don't have an object are called intransitive. Some verbs can only be intransitive (disagree).

In addition they cannot be used in the **Passive Voice** e.g. smile, fall, come, go.

For example:

- David disagreed. – intransitive.

Verbs that have an object are called transitive verbs e.g. eat, drive, give.

For example:

- David **gave** her a present.

Some verbs can be transitive or intransitive e.g. sing

For example:

- Xavier Nadu sings. – intransitive.
- Xavier Nadu sings pop songs. – transitive.

Adverbials

An 'adverbial' or 'adverbial phrase' is a word or expression in the sentence that does the same job as an adverb; that is, it tells you something about how the action in the verb was done.

For example:

- I sometimes have trouble with adverbs.
- He spoke very quietly.
- I've read that book three times.
- She's *gone to the bank*.

The first tells us the frequency of the action (sometimes), the second how he carried out the action (quietly), and the third how many times the action has happened (three).

The fourth is a little different, as in this case the adverbial (gone to the bank) is more or less demanded by the verb (has).

To remember the form of such verbs use your notebooks to write down the different forms.

For example:

- to go [somewhere]
- to put [something][somewhere]

This information is also useful when deciding the order of adverbials in a sentence. Unlike the previous parts of the sentence, a sentence can contain an indefinite number of adverbials, although in practice it's a good idea to keep them few in number.

Complement

A complement is used with verbs like be, seem, look etc. Complements give more information about the subject or, in some structures, about the object.

There are various definitions of 'complement', which range from the very general (anything in the predicate except the verb, including the direct object and adverbs) to the much more restrictive one used here.

A complement is the part of the sentence that gives you more information about the subject (a subject complement) or the object (an object complement) of the sentence.

The complement to be used, if any, is dependent on the verb used in the sentence. Subject complements normally follow certain verbs.

For example:

- He is Spanish.
- She became an engineer.
- That man looks like John.

Object complements follow the direct object of the verb-

For example:

- They painted thc house red.
- She called him an idiot!
- I saw her standing there.

The complement often consists of an adjective or noun phrase, but can also be a participle phrase, as in the last example. It is often not very clear whether a phrase is a complement or an adverbial.

■

Simple Spelling Guide 18

English Spelling!

To speak English well, you need grammar. To write English well, you need grammar, punctuation and spelling.

In Old England words were written as they sounded (phonetically) and so one word could often be spelt in many different ways. In addition English has adopted words from many other languages.

Eventually spelling was standardised, and although many English words have irregular spellings there are some rules that can help you. Watch out though, for every rule there are always some exceptions! English has over 1,100 different ways to spell its 44 separate sounds, more than any other language.

How to Improve Your Spelling?

1. Keep a notebook of words you find difficult to spell. Underline the part of the word that you find most difficult.
2. Use a dictionary, not a spell-checker! OK use a spell-checker, but don't rely on it. Spell-checkers don't check for meaning, the most common misspelt words I have seen on the net are there and their.
3. Learn words with their possible prefixes and suffixes.
4. Learn the rules, but don't rely on them. As I mentioned earlier for every rule there is at least one exception.

For example:

i before e except after c

One of the first English spelling rules learnt in most schools is "i before e except after c". This only works when the pronunciation of the word is like a long ee as in shield.

For example:

piece, relief, niece, priest, thief

but after c

conceive, conceit, receive, receipt

when A or I is the sound

it's the other way round

with an 'a' sound - deign, eight, neighbour, feign, reign, vein, weight

with an 'i' sound either, feisty, height, neither, sleight

Exceptions:

seize, weird, conscientious, conscience, efficient.

Silent Letters

What is a Silent Letter?

A silent letter is a letter that must be included when you write the word even though you don't pronounce it. Over half the alphabet can appear as silent letters in words.

They can be found at the beginning, end or middle of the words and, from the sound of the word, you wouldn't know that they were there.

For example:

a - treadle, bread

b - lamb, bomb, comb

c - scissors, science, scent

d - edge, bridge, ledge

h - honour, honest, school

k - know, knight, knowledge

l - talk, psalm, should

n - hymn, autumn, column

p - pneumatic, psalm, psychology

s - isle, island, aisle

t - listen, rustle, shistle

u - biscuit, guess, guitar

w - write, wrong, wrist

Silent e

Silent e is the most commonly found silent letter in the alphabet.

There are some hard and fast rules for spelling when a word ends with a silent e.

When you wish to add a suffix to a word and it ends with a silent e,

f the suffix begins with a consonant you don't need to change the stem of the word.

For example:

force + ful	=forceful
manage + ment	=management
sincere + ly	=sincerely

If however the suffix begins with a vowel, drop the e before adding the suffix.

For example:

fame + ous	=famous
nerve + ous	=nervous
believable + y	=believably
criticise + ism	=criticism

Exceptions:

mileage, agreeable

Prefixes and Suffixes

Adding a prefix to a word doesn't usually change the spelling of the stem of the word.

For example:

anti + septic	antiseptic
auto + biography	autobiography
de - sensitise	desensitise
dis - approve	disapprove
im - possible	impossible
inter - mediate	intermediate
mega - byte	megabyte
mis - take	mistake
micro - chip	microchip
re - used	reused
un - available	unavailable

Adding a suffix to a word often changes the spelling of the stem of the word. The following may help you work out the changes. Again there are exceptions, so if you're not sure - look it up in your dictionary.

Words ending in a consonant

When the suffix begins with a consonant, just add the ending without any changes.

For example:

treat + ment	treatment

Doubling the Consonant

For most words with a short vowel sound, ending with a single consonant, double the consonant when adding a suffix that starts with a vowel, such as *er*, *ed* or *ing*.

For example:

mop + ing	mopping
big + est	biggest
hot + er	hotter

For words endling in l after a vowel, double the l before adding *er*, *ed* or *ing*.

For example:

carol + ing	carolling
travel + er	travelling

Exceptions:

Some words ending in r, x, w or y are exceptions to the doubling rule

tear + ing	tearing

blow + ing	blowing
box + er	boxer
know + ing	knowing

And if your main word has two consonants at the end, or more than one vowel, don't double the consonant.

Word Endings

Words ending in ce and ge, when you want to add a suffix starting with a or o leave the e in.

For example:

manage + able	manageable
notice + able	noticeable
courage + ous	courageous

Exceptions:

prestige + ous	prestigious

Words ending in ie

When you want to add **ing** to verbs ending in ie, drop the e and change the i to a y.

For example:

die - dying

lie - lying

tie - tying

rain + ing (two vowels a + i)	raining
keep + er (two vowels e + e)	keeper

break + ing (two vowels e + a)	breaking
hang + er (two consonants n + g)	hanger

Words ending in ce and ge

When you want to add a suffix starting with a or o leave the e in.

For example:

manage + able	manageable
notice + able	noticeable
courage + ous	courageous

Exceptions:

prestige + ous	prestigious

Words ending in ie

When you want to add **ing** to verbs ending in ie, drop the e and change the i to a y.

For example:

die - dying

lie - lying

tie - tying

Words ending in y after a consonant

When you want to add suffixes such -as, -ed, -es, -er, -eth, -ly, -ness, -ful and -ous to a word ending in y after a consonant, change the y to an i before adding the suffix.

For example:

eighty + eth	eightieth

duty + es	duties
lazy + ness	laziness
mystery +ous	mysterious
beauty + ful	beautiful
multiply + ed	multiplied
busy + ly	busily

Words ending in y after a vowel

Keep the y when adding suffixes such as er, ing or ed.

For example:

destroy	destroying	destroyed
pry	prying	pried
buy	buying	buyer
play	playing	player

■

The Tenses 19

Tenses

Tenses can show the time of a verb's action or being. The verb ending is changed (conjugated) to show roughly what time it is referring to.

Time can be split into three periods The Present, The Past and The Future.

The tenses are Simple, Continuous and Perfect.

In English we use two tenses to talk about the present and six tenses to talk about the past. There are several ways to talk about the future some of which use the present tenses, these are:

Present	Simple Present
	Present Continuous
Past	Simple Past
	Past Continuous
	Present Perfect Simple
	Present Perfect Continuous
	Past Perfect Simple
	Past Perfect Continuous

Future	Using the Simple Present
	Using the Present Continuous
	Using the Present Perfect Simple
	Using the Present Perfect Continuous
	Using *going to*
	Using *shall/will*

Simple Tenses

The simple tenses are used to show permanent characteristics of people and events or what happens regularly, habitually or in a single completed action.

Continuous Tenses

The continuous tenses are used when talking about a particular point in time.

Perfect Tenses

Sometimes you need to give just a little bit more information about an action or state...and that is where the perfect tenses come in.

The perfect tenses are used when an action or situation in the present is linked to a moment in the past. It is often used to show things that have happened up to now but aren't finished yet or to emphasise that something happened but is not true anymore. When they end determines which of them you use.

Perfect tenses are never used when we say when something happened i.e. yesterday, last year etc. but can be used when discussing the duration of something i.e., often, for, always, since etc.

The Future Tenses

Discussing the future in English can seem complicated.The present simple, present continuous, present perfect simple and the present perfect continuous can all be used and often it is possible to use more than one structure, but have the same meaning.

Simple Present Tense

The Simple Present Tense

The simple present tense is used to discuss permanent situations and the frequency of events.

<table>
<tr><th>To have</th><th colspan="2">Short form</th><th colspan="2">Other Verbs (to work)</th></tr>
<tr><td>I have</td><td colspan="2">I've</td><td colspan="2">I work</td></tr>
<tr><td>he has</td><td colspan="2">he's</td><td colspan="2">He works</td></tr>
<tr><td>she has</td><td colspan="2">she's</td><td colspan="2">She works</td></tr>
<tr><td>it has</td><td colspan="2">it's</td><td colspan="2">It works</td></tr>
<tr><td>you have</td><td colspan="2">you've</td><td colspan="2">you work</td></tr>
<tr><td>we have</td><td colspan="2">we've</td><td colspan="2">we work</td></tr>
<tr><td>they have</td><td colspan="2">they've</td><td colspan="2">they work</td></tr>
<tr><th>Statements +</th><th>Statements -</th><th>Questions</th><th>Short answer +</th><th>Short answer -</th></tr>
<tr><td>I work.</td><td>I don't work.</td><td>Do I work?</td><td>Yes, I do.</td><td>No, I don't.</td></tr>
<tr><td>He works.</td><td>He doesn't work.</td><td>Does he work?</td><td>Yes, he does.</td><td>No, he doesn't.</td></tr>
<tr><td>She works.</td><td>She doesn't work.</td><td>Does she work?</td><td>Yes, she does.</td><td>No, she doesn't.</td></tr>
</table>

It works.	It doesn't work.	Does it work?	Yes, it does.	No, it doesn't.
You work.	You don't work.	Do you work?	Yes you do.	No, you don't.
We work.	We don't work.	Do we work?	Yes we do.	No, we don't.
They work.	They don't work.	Do they work?	Yes they do.	No, they don't.

Regular or Permanent Situations

When something happens regularly or is a permanent situation we usually use the simple present tense. When using the simple present the verb (with the exception of the auxiliary verbs) remains in the dictionary form (verb + s with he/she/it).

Simple Present Timeline

◄…………… I do ……………►

Past — Future

For example:

Q. "Where do you *live*?" A. "I *live* in Germany."

Q. "Where does he *live*?" A. "He *lives* in Germany."

Q. "What *do* you do?" A. "*I'm* a teacher."

Q. "What *does* he do?" A. "*He's* a teacher."

Frequency

The simple present tense is also used to show how often something happens with adverbs of frequency – always, usually, often, sometimes, occasionally, seldom, rarely, never, etc....

And when discussing daily, weekly, monthly etc. routines.

For example:

- "I *always get up* at 6.00."
- "I *never drink* coffee before 12.00."
- "I *work* on my website *every day*."
- "*Every* Monday and Thursday I *go* to the gym."

We also use the simple present to ask for and give instructions or to discuss a series of actions.

For example:

Q. How do I make pancakes?" A. Well, first you take 4 eggs and crack them into a bowl, then you weigh out 4 oz. of flour and sieve it into the eggs etc.

The simple present tense can also be used to discuss future events.

Simple Past Tense

The Simple Past Tense

The simple past tense is used to talk about actions that happened at a specific time in the past. You state when it happened using a time adverb.

You form the simple past of a verb by adding -ed onto the end of a regular verb but, irregular verb forms have to be learned.

To be Statements +	**To be Statements -**	**Questions?**
I was.	I wasn't.	Was I?
He was.	He wasn't.	Was he?

She was.	She wasn't.	Was she?
It was.	It wasn't.	Was it?
You were.	You weren't.	Were you?
We were.	We weren't.	Were we?
They were.	They weren't.	Were they?

Regular Verb (to work) Statements +	**Regular Verb (to work) Statements -**	**Questions**	**Short answer +**	**Short answer -**
I worked.	I didn't work.	Did I work?	Yes, I did.	No, I didn't.
He worked.	He didn't work.	Did he work?	Yes, he did.	No, he didn't.
She worked.	She didn't work.	Did she work?	Yes, she did.	No, she didn't.
It worked.	It didn't work.	Did it work?	Yes, it did.	No, it didn't.
You worked.	You didn't work.	Did you work?	Yes you did.	No, you didn't.

We worked.	We didn't work.	Did we work?	Yes we did.	No, we didn't.
They worked.	They didn't work.	Did they work?	Yes they did.	No, they didn't.

Simple Past Timeline

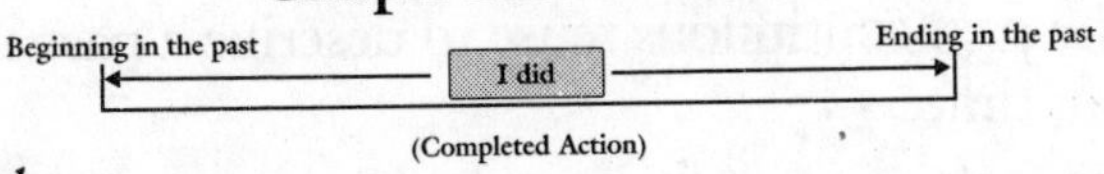

For example:

- "*Last year* I *took* my exams."
- "I *got* married in *1992*."

It can be used to describe events that happened over a period of time in the past but not now.

For example:

- "I *lived* in South Africa *for two years*."

The simple past tense is also used to talk about habitual or repeated actions that took place in the past.

For example:

- "*When I was a child* we always *went* to the seaside on bank holidays."

Simple Future Tense

The Simple Future Tense

We sometimes use the simple present form to discuss future events. Especially when talking about official events that happen at a set time such as timetables, meetings, itineraries, programmes etc.

For example:

Q. "What time does the train leave?" A. "It leaves at 17.30."

Q. "What time does the meeting begin tomorrow?" A. "It begins at 8.00 am."

Q. "What time do you arrive at the airport tomorrow?" A. "I arrive at 6.30 pm."

Past Continuous Tense

The Past Continuous

We use the past continuous tense to describe a past action over a period of time.

Past Continuous Timeline

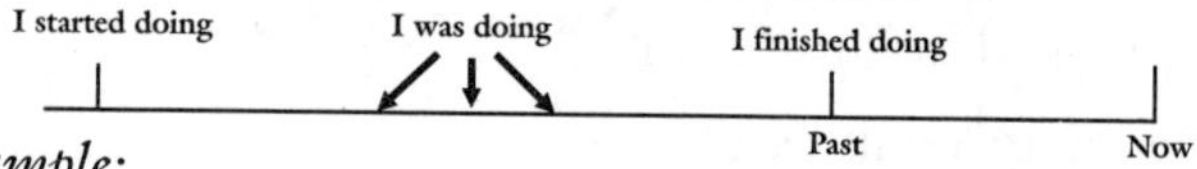

For example:

Q. "What *were* they *doing* yesterday?" A. "They *were working* all day."

It can be used to describe what someone was doing at a particular point in time.

For example:

Q. "What *were* you *doing* at 7.30 last night?" A. "I *was watching* television."

The past continuous can also be used to show that an activity frequently took place over a period of time.

Q. "What *did* you do on holiday?" A. "I *went skiing* a lot."

Often the past continuous is mixed with the past simple to show what was happening when something happened. The past continuous refers to the longer event and the simple past to the event that interrupted it.

For example:

- "I *was driving* to work *when I crashed* my car."

or

- As I *was driving* to work, *I crashed* my car."

Present Continuous Tense

The Present Continuous Tense

When we talk about events that are actually happening now, we use the present continuous tense.

Statements +	**Statements -**	**Questions**	**Short answer +**	**Short answer -**
I'm working.	I'm not working.	Am I working?	Yes, I am.	No, I'm not.
He's working.	He isn't working.	Is he working?	Yes, he is.	No, he isn't.
She's working.	She isn't working.	Is she working?	Yes, she is.	No, she isn't.
It's working.	It isn't working.	Is it working?	Yes, it is.	No, it isn't.
You're working.	You aren'tt working.	Are you working?	Yes you are.	No, you aren't.
We're working.	We aren't working.	Are we working?	Yes we are.	No, we aren't.
They're working.	They aren't working.	Are they working?	Yes they are.	No, they aren't.

Present Continuous Timeline

For example:

Q. "What are you doing?" A. "I'm building a website."

We also use the present continuous tense to talk about things that are happening around now but are temporary.

For example:

Q. "What are you *doing* these days?" A. "Unfortunately I'm *working* a lot."

It is also used to describe trends or situations that are happening but may be temporary.

For example:

- "Nowadays more and more people are *shopping* on the Internet."
- ...and habitual actions (usually negative).

For example:

- "He's always *cleaning* his car."

The present continuous tense can also be used to discuss future events:

Note: The present continuous is usually used with doing verbs (verbs of action) not with verbs of state. The following verbs are **not** used in the continuous form:

Conditions: belong, cost, need, own, seem

Feelings: like, love, hate, want, wish

Beliefs: believe, feel, kn ow, mean, remember, think, understand

Future Continuous Tense

The Future Continuous Tense

The present continuous tense is often used to ask about and discuss future arrangements or plans with just the addition of a future time, but only when these arrangements are certain.

For example:

Q. What are you *doing next week*?"

A. "I'm *working*."

Q. What's he *doing tomorrow*?"

A. "He's *playing* tennis."

The present continuous tense is also used to talk about and make future appointments and arrangements using the words go or come....

For example:

Q. When are you *coming* to see me?"

A. "Next week."

Q. What are you *doing* tomorrow?"

A. "I'm *going* to the dentist."

...and using verbs of arrival and departure.

- "We're *arriving* in London at 2.30."
- "The train *leaving* from platform one is the 2.45 to Edinburgh."

The Future Continuous (will be doing)

The use of 'will be doing' in a sentence is often referred to as the future continuous. It is used to talk about activities that will be happening at a particular time or over a particular time in the future.

For example:

Next week we *will be having* a party. Can you come?

You can also use it (or the present continuous form) to talk about future plans.

For example:

We *will be leaving* here at 7.30 pm.

The Past Perfect Simple Tense

The past perfect simple tense is used to go further back in time when we are already talking about the past. It can make it clear that something had already happened at the time we are talking about.

Past Perfect Simple Timeline

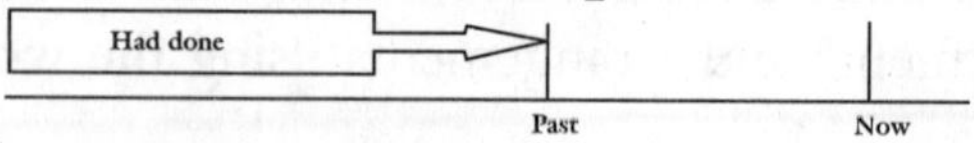

We form the past perfect simple by using the auxilliary verb had and the -ed form of the regular verb (the past participle) irregular verb forms have to be learned:

Statements +	Statements -	Questions	Short answer +	Short answer -
I'd worked...	I hadn't worked...	Had I worked...?	Yes, I had.	No, I hadn't.
He'd worked...	He hadn't worked...	Had he worked...?	Yes, he had.	No, he hadn't.
She'd worked...	She hadn't worked...	Had she worked...?	Yes, she had.	No, she hadn't.
It had worked...	It hadn't worked...	Had it worked...?	Yes, it had.	No, it hadn't.
You'd worked...	You hadn't worked...	Had you worked...?	Yes you had.	No, you hadn't.
We'd worked...	We hadn't worked...	Had we worked...?	Yes we had.	No, we hadn't.
They'd worked...	They hadn't worked...	Had they worked...?	Yes they had.	No, they hadn't.

For example:

- "I *had already done* the shopping by the time she *came* home."
- "I *was* late for work, by the time I *arrived* the client *had already left*."

The past perfect simple can be used to show how often something happened in the past.

For example:

- *I'd visited* the city *many times* before.
- *I'd visited* the city *many times* before.

It can also be used to express unfulfilled wishes or dreams. Sometimes called the Third Conditional.

For example:

- "*If I had won* the lottery *I would have bought* a new car." *Note: If I had done something I would have done something else.*

The Past Perfect Continuous Tense

The past perfect continuous tense is used to talk about longer situations that continued up to the moment in the past we are talking about.

Past Perfect Continuous Timeline

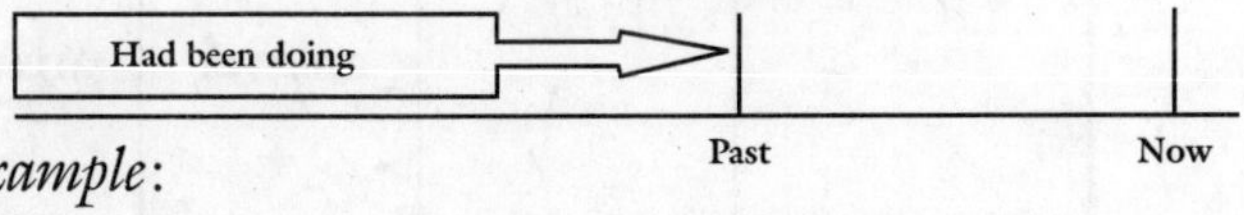

For example:

- "By the time I *left* England we *had been living* in Bristol for five years."
- "His back *was sore* because he *had been sitting* at the computer all day."

It is also used to say how long something went on for up to a past time.

For example:

- We apologised because *we had kept them* waiting *for 3 hours.*
- We apologised because *we had kept them* waiting *since lunchtime.*

The Present Perfect Simple Tense

The present perfect simple tense is used to talk about a past time, which has very strong meaning for the present.

Present Perfect Simple Timeline

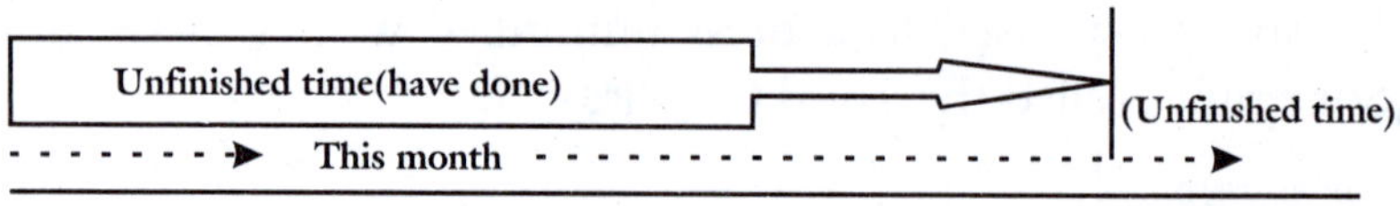

For example:

Q. Where's Jane?

A. She *has gone out*. She should be back in an hour.

We form the present perfect simple by using the auxilliary verb have/has and the -ed form of the regular verb (the past participle) irregular verb forms have to be learned:

Statements +	Statements -	Questions	Short answer +	Short answer -
I've worked.	I haven't worked.	Have I worked?	Yes, I have.	No, I haven't.
He's worked.	He hasn't worked.	Has he worked?	Yes, he has.	No, he hasn't.

She's worked.	She hasn't worked.	Has she worked?	Yes, she has.	No, she hasn't.
It's worked.	It hasn't worked.	Has it worked?	Yes, it has.	No, it hasn't.
You've worked.	You haven't worked.	Have you worked?	Yes you have.	No, you haven't.
We've worked.	We haven't worked.	Have we worked?	Yes we have.	No, we haven't.
They've worked.	They haven't worked.	Have they worked?	Yes they have.	No, they haven't.

The present perfect simple is used to discuss events that have just been completed at the moment of speaking.

For example:

Q. Have you done your homework?"

A. "Yes, I've just finished it."

It is often used to suggest that a past action still has an effect upon something happening in the present.

For example:

- "The pound has fallen against the dollar."

  It is also used to discuss unfinished time.

For example:

Q. Have you done your homework today?

A. No, I haven't done it yet.

Note: You are talking about today and today isn't finished, so you can do your homework later!

Q. Have you ever been to England?"

A. "Yes I have."

Note: You are talking about something that has happened in your life and your life isn't finished!

You can also use the present perfect to discuss something from the past but you don't want to say exactly when.

For example:

Q. "Are you learning any languages?"

A. "Yes, I've begun to learn English."

This tense is often used to discuss events that have been happening over a period of time, but aren't finished yet.

For example:

Q. "How long *have* you *studied* English for?"

A. "I*'ve studied* English for 2 years now."

However it is better (grammatically speaking) to use the Present Perfect Continuous to express yourself in this way.

For example:

Q. "How long *have* you *been studying* English for?"

A. "I*'ve been studying* English *for* 2 years now."

The Present Perfect Continuous Tense

The present perfect continuous tense is often used (with for or since) to describe how long something has been happening up to now.

Present Perfect Continuous Timeline

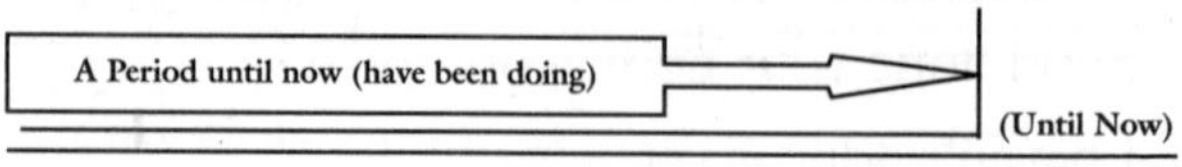

For example:

Q. How long have you been studying English?"

A. I've been studying English **for** four years."

Note: You can just say "**For** four years."

Q. How long have you been living in Germany?

A. I've been living here **since** 1998.

Note: You can just say "**Since** 1998".

The present perfect continuous is also used to refer to an event that may or may not be finished when it's effect can be seen now.

For example:

- Look! It's been snowing.

Note: It's not necessarily snowing now but you can see the effect (the snow on the ground).

You should also use the present perfect continuous when talking about how long you have been doing your current job or working on unfinished projects:

For example:

- I have been working at BT **for** three years.
- We have been exporting to China **since** 1999.

The Present Perfect Future Tense

Discussing the future using the present perfect simple form.

You can use the present perfect simple form to say that something will have happened by a certain time in the future.

"This time next year I *will have finished* my exams."

Discussing the future using the present perfect continuous

form (also known as the future perfect continuous using will have been doing).

You can use the present perfect continuous form to say how long something will have been happening by a certain time in the future.

"This time next year I *will have been teaching* English for 9 years."

The Present Perfect Future Tense

Discussing the future using the present perfect simple form.

You can use the present perfect simple form to say that something will have happened by a certain time in the future.

"This time next year I *will have finished* my exams."

Discussing the future using the present perfect continuous form (also known as the future perfect continuous using will have been doing).

You can use the present perfect continuous form to say how long something will have been happening by a certain time in the future.

"This time next year I will have been teaching English for 9 years."

Future Tense

Discussing the future using *going to*

We say something is going to happen when it has already been planned.

For example:

Q. Are you going to fly to Germany?

A. No, we're going to drive.

We also use it to show something has already been decided.

For example:

- "We're going to buy a new car next year."

We also use going to when we can see something is about to happen.

For example:

- "Look at that cloud. I think it's going to rain."
- "Watch out! He's going to crash into that tree!"

You can also use *going to* to predict the future based upon the evidence now.

For example:

- "It looks as though Mohan Bagan are going to win the Durand cup.
- "I think my friend Ramesh is going to have a baby."
- Thanks to Brijesh for pointing out the following:
- "I'm going to Germany." isn't really the future tense. You would have to say "I'm ***going to go to*** Germany."

Discussing the future using *shall/will*

When we give information about the future or predict future events that are not certain we usually use shall/will.

For example:

Q. Who do you think *will win* the election?"

A. "I'm not sure but I think the current party *will win*."

We can also use shall/will to make promises for the future.

When leaving work I would say – "Goodnight, *I'll* (I will) see you tomorrow."

Shall/Will is often used when we just decide to do something.

For example:

The phone is ringing – If I decide to answer the phone I would say – "*I'll* (I will) get it."

It can also be used in formal situations to express planned events and is preferred in formal written English.

For example:

The party *will start* at 10.00 pm.

■

Verbs – An Overview 20

Verbs are a class of words used to show the performance of an action (do, throw, run), existence (be), possession (have), or state (know, love) of a subject. To put it simply a verb shows what something or someone does.

Most statements in speech and writing have a main verb. These verbs are expressed in tenses which place everything in a point in time.

Verbs are conjugated (inflected) to reflect how they are used. There are two general areas in which conjugation occurs; for person and for tense.

Conjugation for tense is carried out on all verbs. All conjugations start with the infinitive form of the verb. The infinitive is simply the *to* form of the verb. For example, ***to begin***. The present participle form (the-ing form), is formed by adding *ing* to the bare infinitive.

For example, the present participle of the verb *to begin* is *beginning*. There are two other forms that the verb can take, depending on the tense type and time, the simple past form (*began*) and the past participle (*begun*).

Conjugation for person occurs when the verb changes form, depending on whether it is governed by a first, second, or third person subject. This gives three conjugations for any verb depending on who is acting as the subject of the verb. For example, we have: *to begin, you begin,* and *he begins.* Note that only the third conjunction really shows a difference.

While most English verbs simply do not show extensive conjugation forms for person, an exception is the verb *to be.*

Action Verbs

Action verbs are verbs that show the performance of an action. They are dynamic verbs that show something happening.

There are regular and irregular action verbs.

For example:

- *To walk* is a regular action verb
- *To run* is an irregular action verb

Auxiliary Verbs

Auxiliary verbs are used together with a main verb to give grammatical information and therefore add extra meaning to a sentence, which is not given by the main verb.

They are used to form the passive voice.

They are used to form the continuous tense.

They are used to form the perfect tense.

Be, Do and Have are auxiliary verbs, they are irregular verbs and can be used as main verbs. The verbs 'to be' and 'to have' are the most commonly used auxiliary verbs and work alongside the main verbs in any statement.

Modal verbs are also auxiliary verbs, but will be treated separately, these are can, could, may, might, must, shall, should, will, and would, they differ from the others in that they can never function as a main verb.

To be

Be is the most common verb in the English language. It can be used as an auxiliary and a main verb. It is used a lot in its other forms.

Base form = *be*

Present form = *am/is/are*

Past form = *was/were*

Present Participle / Gerund = *being*

Past Participle = *been*

To do

The verb do is one of the most common verbs in English. It can be used as an auxiliary and a main verb. It is often used in questions.

Base form = *do*

Present form = *do/does*

Past form = *did*

Present Participle / Gerund = *doing*

Past Participle = *done*

To have

Have is one of the most common verbs in the English language.

Base form = *have*

Present form = *have / has*

Past form = *had*

Present Participle / Gerund = *having*

Past Participle = *had*

Verbs – Finite/Non-finite

Finite Verbs

A finite verb (sometimes called main verbs) is a verb that has a subject, this means that it can be the main verb in a sentence. It shows tense (past/present etc) or number (singular/plural).

For example:

I lived in Germay. (*I* is the subject - *lived* describes what the subject did - *lived* is a finite verb).

Non-finite Verbs

A non-finite verb has no subject, tense or number. The only non-finite verb forms are the infinitive (indicated by to), the gerund or the participle.

For example:

I lived in Germany to improve my German. (*To improve* is in the infinitive form – improve is non-finite).

Irregular Verbs

Irregular verbs have no rules for conjugation. These can only be learnt in context - sorry!

They all have a base form. *e.g. to run*

A gerund (ing) form where *ing* is added to the end of the verb. *e.g. running*

An -s form where *s* is added to the end of the verb. *e.g. runs.*

A past tense form which must be learnt. *e.g. ran.*

A past participle form which must be learnt. *e.g. run.*

Modal Verbs

All the auxiliary verbs except be, do and have are called modals. Unlike other auxiliary verbs modals only exist in their helping form; they cannot act alone as the main verb in a sentence.

Be, do, and have also differ from the other auxiliaries in that they can also serve as ordinary verbs in a given sentence.

The Modal verbs are:

CAN / COULD / MAY / MIGHT / MUST / SHALL / SHOULD / OUGHT TO / WILL / WOULD

Modal	Example	Uses
Can	They can control their own budgets. We can't fix it. Can I smoke here? Can you help me?	Ability / Possibility Inability / Impossibility Asking for permission Request
Could	Could I borrow your dictionary? Could you say it again more slowly? We could try to fix it ourselves. I think we could have another Gulf War. He gave up his old job so he could work for us.	Asking for permission. Request Suggestion Future possibility Ability in the past
May	May I have another cup of coffee? China may become a major economic power.	Asking for permission Future possibility
Might	They might give us a 10% discount.	Future possibility

Must	We must say good-bye now. They mustn't disrupt the work more than necessary.	Necessity / Obligation Prohibition
Ought to	We ought to employ a professional writer.	Saying what's right or correct
Shall (More common in the UK than the US)	Shall I help you with your luggage? Shall we say 2.30 then? Shall I do that or will you?	Offer Suggestion Asking what to do
Should	We should sort out this problem at once. I think we should check everything again. Profits should increase next year.	Saying what's right or correct Recommending action Uncertain prediction
Will	I can't see any taxis so I'll walk. I'll do that for you if you like. I'll get back to you first thing on Monday. Profits will increase next year.	Instant decisions Offer Promise Certain prediction

Would	Would you mind if I brought a colleague with me?	Asking for permission
	Would you pass the salt please?	Request
	Would you mind waiting a moment?	Request
	"Would three o`clock suit you?" - "That'd be fine."	Making arrangements
	Would you like to play golf this Friday?	Invitation
	"Would you prefer tea or coffee?" - "I'd like tea please."	Preferences

The verb used to, which is explained here, can also be used like a modal verb

What is a Phrasal Verb?

A phrasal verb is a combination of a verb and preposition, a verb and an adverb, or a verb with both an adverb and a preposition.

A phrasal verb has a meaning which is different from the original verb. That's what makes them fun, but confusing. You may need to try to guess the meaning from the context, or, failing that, look it up in a dictionary.

The adverb or preposition that follows the verb are sometimes called a particle. The particle changes the meaning of the phrasal verb in idiomatic ways.

They are also known as 'compound verbs', 'verb-adverb combinations', 'verb-particle constructions", "two-part words/

verbs' and 'three-part words/verbs' (depending on the number of words).

Phrasal verbs are usually used informally in everyday speech as opposed to the more formal Latinate verbs, such as "to get together" rather than "to congregate", "to put off" rather than "to postpone", or "to get out" rather than "to exit". They should be avoided in academic writing.

Literal usage

Many verbs in English can be combined with an adverb or a preposition, a phrasal verb used in a literal sense with a preposition is easy to understand.

- "He *walked across* the square.

Verb and adverb constructions are also easy to understand when used literally.

- "She opened the shutters and *looked outside*."
- "When he heard the crash, he *looked up*."

An adverb in a literal phrasal verb modifies the verb it is attached to, and a preposition links the subject to the verb.

Idiomatic usage

It is, however, the figurative or idiomatic application in everyday speech which makes phrasal verbs so important:

- "I hope you will *get over* your operation quickly."

The literal meaning of "to get over", in the sense of "to climb over something to get to the other side", is not relevant here. Here "get over" means "recover from" or "feel better".

Transitive and Intransitive Phrasal Verbs

Phrasal verbs also differ in their transitivity or intransitivity in the same way as normal verbs do. A transitive verb always has an object.

For example:

- "Many people walked across the bridge."

"Across" in this sentence is the preposition to "the bridge".

An intransitive verb does not have an object.

For example:

- "When I entered the room he looked up."

"Up" here is an adverb, and does not have an object.

Separable or Inseparable Phrasal Verbs

A further way of considering phrasal verbs is whether they are separable or inseparable. In inseparable verbs, the object comes after the particle.

For example:

- "She *got on* the bus".
- "On weekdays, we *look after* our grandchildren."

Separable verbs have several ways of separating verb, particle and object. Usually, the object comes between verb and particle.

For example:

- "She *looked up* the word in her dictionary."
- "She *looked* it *up* in her dictionary."

However, with some separable verbs, the object can come before or after the particle.

For example:

- "*Switch* the light *off*."
- "*Switch off* the light."
- "*Switch* it *off*."

Regular Verbs

Regular verbs are conjugated to easy to learn rules.

They all have a base form. *e.g. to look*

A gerund (ing) form where *ing* is added to the end of the verb. *e.g. looking*

An -s form where *s* is added to the end of the verb. *e.g. looks*

A past tense form where *ed* is added to the end of the verb. *e.g. looked*

A past participle form where *ed* is added to the end of the verb. *e.g. looked.*

Conjugation and Contraction – In other words, "The short form."

The long and short of it.

Forms of the auxiliary verbs to be, to do and to have:

To be - Simple Present Form

Positive Statement		**Negative Statement**	
Long form	**Short form**	**Long form**	**Short form**
I am	I'm	I am not	I'm not
He is	He's	He is not	He isn't ***or*** He's not
She is	She's	She is not	She isn't ***or*** She's not
It is	It's	It is not	It isn't ***or*** It's not
You are	You're	You are not	You aren't ***or*** You're not

We are	We're	We are not	We aren't *or* We're not
They are	They're	They are not	They're not

To be - Simple Past Form

Positive Statement		**Negative Statement**	
Long form	**Short form**	**Long form**	**Short form**
I was		I was not	I wasn't
He was		He was not	He wasn't
She was		She was not	She wasn't
It was		It was not	It wasn't
You were		You were not	You weren't
We were		We were not	We weren't
They were		They were not	They weren't

To do - Simple Present Form

Positive Statement		Negative Statement	
Long form	**Short form**	**Long form**	**Short form**
I do	---	I do not	I don't
He does		He does not	He doesn't
She does		She does not	She doesn't
It does		It does not	It doesn't
You do		You do not	You don't
We do		We do not	We don't
They do		They do not	They don't

To do - Simple Past Form

Positive Statement		Negative Statement	
Long form	**Short form**	**Long form**	**Short form**
I / he / she / it / you / we / they ***did***	---	I / he / she / it / you / we / they ***did not***	I / he / she / it / you / we / they ***didn't***

To have - Simple Present Form

Positive Statement		**Negative Statement**	
Long form	**Short form**	**Long form**	**Short form**
I have	I've	I have not	I haven't ***or*** I've not
He has	He's	He has not	He hasn't ***or*** He's not
She has	She's	She has not	She hasn't ***or*** She's not
It has	It's	It has not	It hasn't ***or*** It's not
You have	You've	You have not	You haven't ***or*** You've not
We have	We've	We have not	We haven't ***or*** We've not
They have	They've	They have not	They haven't ***or*** They've not

To have - Simple Past Form

Positive Statement		**Negative Statement**	
Long form	**Short form**	**Long form**	**Short form**
I / he / she / it / you / we / they ***had***	I'd he'd she'd it'd you'd we'd they'd	I / he / she / it / you / we / they ***had not***	I hadn't ***or*** I'd not he hadn't ***or*** he'd not she hadn't ***or*** she'd not it hadn't ***or*** it'd not you hadn't ***or*** you'd not we hadn't ***or*** we'd not they hadn't ***or*** they'd not

The long and short forms of the modal verbs can, could, shall, should, must, will and would

Can

Positive Statement		**Negative Statement**	
Long form	**Short form**	**Long form**	**Short form**
I / he / she / it / you / we / they ***can***	---	I / he / she/ it / you / we / they ***cannot***	I / he / she / it / you / we / they ***can't***

Could

Positive Statement		Negative Statement	
Long form	**Short form**	**Long form**	**Short form**
I / he / she / it / you / we / they ***could***	---	I / he / she/ it / you / we / they ***could not***	I / he / she / it / you / we / they ***couldn't***

Must

Positive Statement		Negative Statement	
Long form	**Short form**	**Long form**	**Short form**
I / he / she / it / you / we / they ***must***	---	I / he / she/ it / you / we / they ***must not***	I / he / she / it / you / we / they ***mustn't***

Shall

Positive Statement		Negative Statement	
Long form	**Short form**	**Long form**	**Short form**
I / he / she / it / you / we / they ***shall***	---	I / he / she/ it / you / we / they ***shall not***	I / he / she / it / you / we / they ***shan't***

Should

Positive Statement		Negative Statement	
Long form	**Short form**	**Long form**	**Short form**
I / he / she / it / you / we / they ***should***	---	I / he / she / it / you / we / they ***should not***	I / he / she / it / you / we / they ***shouldn't***

Will

Positive Statement		Negative Statement	
Long form	**Short form**	**Long form**	**Short form**
I / he / she / it / you / we / they ***will***	I'll He'll She'll It'll You'll We'll They'll	I / he / she / it / you / we / they ***will not***	I won't ***or*** I'll not He won't ***or*** He'll not She won't ***or*** She'll not It won't ***or*** It'll not You won't ***or*** You'll not We won't ***or*** We'll not They won't ***or*** They'll not

Would

Positive Statement		Negative Statement	
Long form	Short form	Long form	Short form
I / he / she / it / you / we / they ***would***	I'd He'd She'd It'd You'd We'd They'd	I / he / she / it / you / we / they ***would not***	I wouldn't ***or*** I'd not He wouldn't ***or*** He'd not She wouldn't ***or*** She'd not It wouldn't ***or*** It'd not You wouldn't ***or*** You'd not We wouldn't ***or*** We'd not They wouldn't ***or*** They'd not

21 Active Voice/Passive Voice

What do you mean Voice?

In English grammar, voice shows whether the subject of a sentence is doing the action, or having the action done to it.

The Active Voice

We say things in the active voice when we want to show who or what has done something.

In the active voice the agent (the person or thing that does something) becomes the subject of the sentence.

For example:

"She cleaned the office." (Who cleaned the office? She did=*the subject*)

"He stole my car." (Who stole my car? He did=*the subject*)

The active voice uses fewer words than the pompous sounding passive voice. Some tests often include passive constructions that need revision.

The Passive Voice

The passive voice may use any tense of the verb *to be*:

	To be		Past Participle
I / It / They etc.	is / are / am was / were	(present simple) (past simple)	finished.
I / It / They etc.	is being / are being /am being was being / were being	(present continuous) (past continuous)	cleaned.
I / It / They etc.	has been / have been had been	(present perfect) (past perfect)	sent.
I / It / They etc.	will be	(future)	tired.

The passive voice is used when the subject of a sentence is the person or thing affected by the action of the sentence. We particularly use the passive voice when we don't know or aren't bothered exactly who has done something. This is called passive without agent where the recipient of the action becomes the subject.

For example:

"The office was cleaned." (What was cleaned? - The office=*the subject*)

We often use the passive to report what someone has said but we want to avoid telling anyone who said it.

For example:

"I was told you weren't coming."

Sometimes it is used in order to deliberately avoid saying who did something, or more often who's to blame for something. Either because you don't know, or because you don't want to say. You'll often see it used in politics, the business world, or in any other activity involving bureaucracy.

"The civilian was shot." (Who was shot? The civilian=*the subject*)

"The report was mislaid." (What was mislaid? The report =*the subject*)

Sometimes you may want to use the passive voice but wish to mention who carried out the action. This is called passive with agent and the agent is usually introduced with the word *by*.

For example:

"The office was cleaned *by* Mrs Rosy."

Or you may use a subject such as people, someone, they etc, when you don't know who the agent is.

For example:

"The car was stolen *by* joyriders."

When you can't use the Passive

Intransitive verbs cannot be used in the passive. This is because they cannot have objects, and so there is nothing to become the subject of the passive sentence. For example with verbs like *die* or *arrive*.

■

Vocabulary 22

Telling the Time

Asking the Time

Here are some phrases you can use when you want to know the time:

- What's the time?
- What time is it?
- Have you got the right time?
- What time do you make it?

Telling the Time

To tell someone what the time is, we can say "The time is..." or, more usually, "It's...". Here is a typical dialogue:

Question: What's the time, please?

Answer: It's three o'clock.

The chart below shows you two different ways to tell someone what the time is.

	It's...	It's...
3.00	three o'clock	three
3.02	*just gone three o'clock*	three oh two

3.03	three *minutes* past three	three oh three
3.05	five past three	three oh five
3.09	nine *minutes* past three	three oh nine
3.10	ten past three	three ten
3.15	a quarter past three	three fifteen
3.20	twenty past three	three twenty
3.21	twenty-one *minutes* past three	three twenty-one
3.25	twenty-five past three	three twenty-five
3.30	half past three	three thirty
3.35	twenty-five to four	three thirty-five
3.40	twenty to four	three forty
3.45	a quarter to four	three forty-five
3.50	ten to four	three fifty
3.55	five to four	three fifty-five
3.57	three *minutes* to four	three fifty-seven
3.58	*nearly four c'clock*	three fifty-eight
4.00	four o'clock	four

Day and Night

There are 24 hours in a day. The day is divided into "day(time)" and "night(-time)". Daytime is from sunrise (this varies, but we can say approximately 6 am) to sunset (we can say approximately 6 pm). Night-time is from sunset to sunrise.

Every day starts precisely at midnight. AM (Ante-Meridiem = before noon) starts **just after** midnight. PM (Post-Meridiem = after noon) starts **just after** midday. This means that 12 am and 12 pm have no meaning.

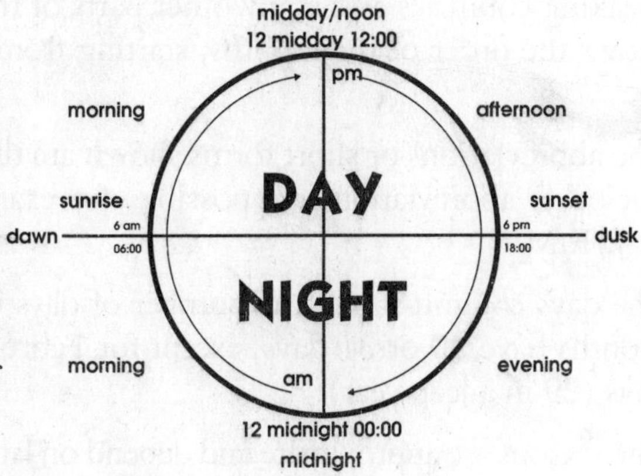

This diagram shows the cycle of a 24-hour day and the words we use to describe its parts. The day starts at midnight (at the bottom of the diagram).

Days of the Week

Notice that "weekdays" and "days of the week" are not the same. "Days of the week" are all 7 days from Monday to Sunday. "Weekdays" are only the 5 days from Monday to Friday. The "weekend" is Saturday and Sunday.

	Day	**Abbreviation**	
Weekdays	Monday	Mon.	Mo.
	Tuesday	Tue.	Tu.
	Wednesday	Wed.	We.
	Thursday	Thu.	Th.
	Friday	Fri.	Fr.

Weekend	Saturday	Sat.	Sa.
	Sunday	Sun.	Su.

Months of the Year

The list below shows the months of the year used in English-speaking countries and many other parts of the world. The list shows the order of the months, starting from January (month 1).

The abbreviations or short forms shown are the most common, but other abbreviations are possible, for example: Ja./Fe./Ma. or J./F./M.

The days column shows the number of days in the month. All months have 30 or 31 days, except for February which has 28 days (29 in a leap year).

The seasons are approximate and depend on latitude. Some parts of the world have only three seasons. The seasons shown here are for the North Temperate Zone (for example North America). In the southern hemisphere, the seasons are reversed.

	Month	Short Form	Days	Season
1	January	Jan.	31	Winter
2	February	Feb.	28/29	
3	March	Mar.	31	Spring
4	April	Apr.	30	
5	May	May	31	

6	June	Jun.	30	Summer
7	July	Jul.	31	
8	August	Aug.	31	
9	September	Sep.	30	Autumn
10	October	Oct.	31	
11	November	Nov.	30	
12	December	Dec.	31	Winter

Writing the Date

There are several different ways to write the date in English. They vary from formal to informal, and there are differences between British and American English. The following table shows some typical formats.

Format	British: Day-Month-Year	American: Month-Day-Year
A	the Fourteenth of March, 1999	March the Fourteenth, 1999
B	14th March 1999	March 14th, 1999
C	14 March 1999	March 14, 1999
D	14/3/1999	3/14/1999

E	14/3/99	3/14/99
F	14/03/99	03/14/99

Note: which format to use is a question of formality, politeness and personal choice. Generally, the longer formats, such as B or C, are more polite (since they show more respect for the reader). Shorter formats, such as D or E, are used in less formal situations, for example a memo, a letter between friends or an impersonal business letter. Format F is rather official and is typically seen on an invoice or an official or technical document. Format A is extremely formal and mainly used on printed items, for example a wedding invitation. The numerical formats may use a full stop (.) or hyphen (-) instead of a slash (/), for example: 14.3.1999 or 03-14-99.

Months			
Number	Name	Abbreviations	
1	January	Jan	J
2	February	Feb	F
3	March	Mar	M
4	April	Apr	A
5	May	May	M
6	June	Jun	J
7	July	Jul	J

8	August	Aug	A
9	September	Sep	S
10	October	Oct	O
11	November	Nov	N
12	December	Dec	D

Days of the Month	
1st	first
2nd	second
3rd	third
4th	fourth
5th	fifth
6th	sixth
7th	seventh
8th	eighth
9th	ninth
10th	tenth

11th	eleventh
12th	twelfth
13th	thirteenth
14th	fourteenth
15th	fifteenth
16th	sixteenth
17th	seventeenth
18th	eighteenth
19th	nineteenth
20th	twentieth
21st	twenty-first
22nd	twenty-second
23rd	twenty-third
24th	twenty-fourth
25th	twenty-fifth
26th	twenty-sixth

27th	twenty-seventh
28th	twenty-eighth
29th	twenty-ninth
30th	thirtieth
31st	thirty-first

Everyday Life

There are three branches of Government.

He came to live with his brother.

He has a very big dog.

He knows how to ride a bike.

He wanted to find a job.

He wanted to talk to his boss.

He went to the post office.

His wife is at work right now.

His wife worked in the house.

I am too busy to talk today.

I bought a blue car today.

I came to _______ (city) today for my interview.

I count the cars as they pass by the office.

I drive a blue car to work.

I go to work everyday.

I have three children.

I know how to speak English.

I live in the State of ___________.

I want to be a United States citizen.

It is a good job to start with.

My car does not work.

She can speak English very well.

She cooks for her friends.

She is my daughter, and he is my son.

She needs to buy some new clothes.She wanted to live near her brother.

She was happy with her house.

The boy threw a ball.

The children bought a newspaper.

The children play at school.

The children wanted a television.

The man wanted to get a job.

The teacher was proud of her class.

The white house has a big tree.

They are a very happy family.

They are very happy with their car.

They buy many things at the store.

They came to live in the United States.

They go to the grocery store.

They have horses on their farm.

They live together in a big house.

They work well together.

Today I am going to the store.

Today is a sunny day.

Warm clothing was on sale in the store.

We are very smart to learn this.

We have a very clean house.

You cook very well.

You drink too much coffee.

You work very hard at your job.

■

23 Sample Conversations

Everything went like clockwork!!!

Monica: I've just popped in to thank you very much for organising last weekend's trip to the seaside for the old folk.

Jyoti: That's very kind of you. They all seemed to enjoy it.

Monica: They certainly did. **Everything went like clockwork**, in fact I don't think you could have done it better.

Jyoti: I'm not sure about that, there were one or two things that could have been improved.

Monica: In a perfect world perhaps, but as far as I'm concerned it was a great success. So thank you again.

You've done a fantastic job!!!

Dhiraj: I've just been reading through your last project report.

Amit: I hope you didn't find too much wrong with it.

Dhiraj: On the contrary, **you've done a fantastic job**.

Amit: Well, I'm not sure about that.

Dhiraj: You're too modest. It's really well organized and written and offers some very well thought out conclusions.

Amit: Well, I'm glad you like it and hope it proves useful.

You look really chic!!!

Geeta: Where are you off to?

Ali: I'm going to a civic reception at the town hall.

Geeta: Who's it for?

Ali: It's for a delegation from our sister city in India.

Geeta: Well I must say that outfit really suits you. **You look really chic.**

Ali: Thank you. I want to look my best for the guests.

It's a cross!!!

Asha: Have you seen Peter's new dog?

Latika: Yes I have but couldn't recognise the breed.

Asha: That's not surprising because it's not a thoroughbred, it's a mongrel.

Latika: Ah, that explains it. What kind of a mixture is it?

Asha: I think **it's a cross** between a collie and a retriever.

Latika: If that's the case it should be a very good-natured dog.

Kittens are always playful!!!

Raju: Look at your brother playing with the kitten.

Latika: Yes, he really enjoys teasing her with that piece of string.

Raju: He's holding it up so she has to jump for it.

Latika: Kittens are always playful, aren't they?

Raju: Yes they are, that's why they're such fun.

Latika: It's a pity they seem to lose much of their playfulness when they get older.

It's very attached to him!!!

Ashok: I'm sorry that the parrot is squawking its head off.

Ravi: What's the matter with it?

Ashok: Well it's just spotted a cat outside the window and it really doesn't like cats.

Ravi: Do you ever let it out of its cage?

Ashok: My father does. **It's very attached to him** so it perches on his shoulder and behaves itself when he's around.

Ravi: Would you ever let it out?

Ashok: Oh no, because it's more than likely to give me a nasty nip if I do.

You have to walk a dog every day!!!

Rajiv: Why is your dog whining and looking at you so expectantly?

Bobby: It's the time of day. He always does that around now.

Rajiv: What does he want?

Bobby: He wants me to take him out for a walk.

Rajiv: Are you going to?

Bobby: Oh yes, but I like to tease him a bit by pretending not to notice.

Rajiv: Do you take him out every day?

Bobby: Of course, **you have to walk a dog every day** because it needs the exercise to stay healthy.

We had to have our cat put to sleep!!!

Richa: What's the matter, you look as if you've been crying?

Sonia: I have, I've just come from the vet's.

Richa: What happened?

Sonia: **We had to have our cat put to sleep**. She had a tumour which was incurable.

Richa: Oh dear! I'm really sorry to hear that. How old was she?

Sonia: She was 15, which is quite old for a cat. But she really was like one of the family. That's why we're all so upset.

That was for the best!!!

Mohit: The parents of children in our street are a lot less worried these days.

Mukesh: Why's that?

Mohit: One of the neighbours had a very fierce dog which scared everyone. Last week it bit one of the children so badly, she had to be treated in hospital.

Mukesh: That must have been an awful experience for the little girl. But why did you say they are not worried now?

Mohit: Well they complained about the dog to the police and the police forced the owner to put it down.

Mukesh: Oh I see. Well I'm sure **that was for the best.**

We must keep him on a leash!!!

Anita: I'm really enjoying this walk in the country and so is the dog.

Rahul: Yes, he's running here, there and everywhere.

Anita: Oh look, there are sheep in the next field!

Rahul: I'll grab him straight away and put him on the leash. Here boy!

Anita: Thank goodness you managed to catch him before he spotted the sheep and started chasing them.

Rahul: Yes, **we must keep him on leash** from now on. Farmers around here are likely to shoot on sight any dogs they catch worrying their sheep.

That's my aim!!!

Danny: I've just had a great piece of luck.

Rajesh: Don't tell me you've won the lottery this week.

Danny: Not quite, I've got a free weekly riding lesson at the local riding stables.

Rajesh: I know you love horses. How did you manage that?

Danny: I offered to muck out the stables and to help groom the horses for four hours every week.

Rajesh: That's not a bad bargain. It won't be long before you're an accomplished horseman if you can keep the arrangement going for any length of time.

Danny: That's my aim.

To be neutered!!!

Monica: Can I see the new kittens?

Rakesh: Of course, they're over here with their mother in this basket.

Monica: There are five! Aren't they tiny and so sweet?

Rakesh: Yes, they're only a few hours old and their eyes haven't opened yet.

Monica: Is this the mother cat's first litter?

Rakesh: Yes it is, and happily they all seem to be healthy.

Monica: Do you expect her to have more in the future?

Rakesh: No, we'll be taking her to the vet **to be neutered** as soon as she has recovered from the birth.

He's got a taste for exotic pets!!!

Harsh: I'm always a bit apprehensive about visiting Pritam.

Priya: Why's that? He's such a nice chap.

Harsh: He is, but **he's got a taste for exotic pets.**

Priya: I didn't know that, such as?

Harsh: Well, last week when I was there he had a baby iguana running around the place.

Priya: A lizard! Ugh, that would give me the creeps.

Harsh: It's not my idea of a pet. But that's not the only thing he's got. He's had a three-foot python for quite a while now as well.

Priya: He ought to get a job in a zoo.

They get out of condition!!!

Ramesh: You're out exercising your dog I see.

Rajiv: Yes, dogs have to be exercised daily, otherwise **they get out of condition.**

Ramesh: What's his name?

Rajiv: Rover.

Ramesh: That's a good name for a dog. Why is he woofing and wagging his tail?

Rajiv: Can't you see? He wants one of us to throw that stick as far as we can for him to fetch.

Ramesh: I can't disappoint him. Come on boys, (throw stick) go fetch!

Our cat had a litter!!!

Arti: What a playful litter kitten! Is it a boy or a girl?

Supriya: It's a girl. We've decided to call her Winkie.

Arti: How sweet! How old is she?

Supriya: Only six weeks.

Arti: Did you get her from a pet shop?

Supriya: No, **our cat had a litter** for four and she's the only one left.

Arti: What do you mean?

Supriya: Well we've given the other three to friends but decided to keep her, as she was the prettiest of the bunch.

He's a thoroughbred Boxer with an outstanding pedigree!!!

Ramesh: Is that your new dog?

Rohit: Yes, we've only had him a week.

Ramesh: He's really handsome and very lively.

Rohit: He should be, he cost a fortune.

Ramesh: Why was he so expensive?

Rohit: He's a thoroughbred Boxer with an outstanding pedigree that's why. We got him from a top breeder.

Ramesh: Do you intend to show him?

Rohit: We're not sure; we'll take a breeder's advice on that.

She is impossible to please!!!

First clerk: I've just had a terrible hour and a half.

Second clerk: Why, what happened?

First clerk: Well I had a lady customer come in who wanted to buy a pair of shoes. And you know we've got a really good range.

Second clerk: We certainly do. Did she buy a pair?

First clerk: No, but she didn't leave before getting me to bring her every single pair we had in the shop. And she complained about every single one.

Second clerk: I'd say **she was impossible to please.**

I haggled him down to Rs 1200!!!

Deepak: I like your new anorak, it looks really expensive, where did you get it – in that upscale sports shop in the mall?

Ramesh: Well thanks, but no I didn't. I got it in the market.

Deepak: How much did you pay for it?

Ramesh: Not as much as the man asked for. He wanted Rs 1800.

Deepak: That would have been a bit steep, it's almost the shop price.

Ramesh: I know, but **I haggled him down to Rs 1200**, so I reckon I've got a bit of a bargain.

I've got it on thirty days' free trial!!!

Aamir: Why are you talking to your computer. Is it lonely?

Dinesh: No, don't be silly, I'm trying out some new speech recognition software.

Aamir: How does it work?

Dinesh: Well, I just speak what I want to say into the microphone and my words appear on the screen. It's magic!

Aamir: It must be very expensive.

Dinesh: It's not cheap but I haven't actually paid anything yet.

Aamir: How come?

Dinesh: I've got it on thirty days' free trial. If I'm not satisfied with it, I can return it free of charge as long as I do so within 30 days.

Have you got them in my size?

Kitty: Excuse me, could you show me to the skirts section please?

Sales girl: Certainly madam, please come this way..

Kitty: Ah! these are just what I've been looking for. **Have you got them in my size?** I'm a size 8.

Sales girl: Just a moment.....! I'm afraid not madam. We appear to be temporarily out of stock.

Kitty: Oh, how disappointing! When will you next have some in?

Sales girl: We should be getting a delivery at the beginning of next week.

My feet are killing me!!!

Geeta: You look a bit tired. What have you been doing?

Preeti: Shopping for some new outfits.

Geeta: Did you get what you want?

Preeti: I did, but it took me all day.

Geeta: What do you want to do now?

Preeti: I just want to sit down somewhere and relax. **My feet are killing me!**

You've been ripped off!!!

Tarun: What do you think of my new suit?

Ajay: Not bad. I like the wide lapels and the pant cuffs. It reminds me of one I saw in the department store the other day. Did you get it there?

Tarun: No, I got it at that new outfitters on the main street.

Ajay: How much did it cost?

Tarun: Five thousand and fifty rupees.

Ajay: What? You could have got the one from the department store for Rs. 3550. **You've been ripped off!**

What a bargain!!!

Harpreet: Look what I've got.

Ravi: Wow, that's the snazziest looking handbag I've ever seen. Where did you get it?

Harpreet: I got it in Paris on my last trip.

Ravi: I bet it cost a fortune?

Harpreet: No it didn't, I got it for half price because the shop was having a clearance sale.

Ravi: What a bargain! You'll have to take me with you next time.

She's got a really useful right foot!!!

Raju: My sister's really keen on soccer.

Rajiv: Really, what team does she support.

Raju: She doesn't support any in particular. When I say keen, I mean she's an enthusiastic player. She plays for a local women's team.

Rajiv: Is she any good?

Raju: Well, she's scored ten goals so far this season. She's got a really useful right foot.

Rajiv: Well if that's the case, you really must take me to see her play sometime.

My sister's hobby is dress making!!!

Neeta: You look slimmer than when I saw you last.

Seema: Yes, I must have lost six pounds over the last two months. my best dress is now too big for me.. I can't wear it any more.

Neeta: Don't say that, I think I can help you.

Seema: How do you mean?

Neeta: Well, my sister's hobby is dress making and I'm sure she wouldn't mind taking it in so that it'll fit you again. I'll ask her.

Seema: That would be fantastic. I'm no good at sewing myself.

She's got a really green thumb!!!

Dhiraj: What a beautiful garden your parents have!

Sujata: I'm glad you like it. They certainly spend a lot of time on it.

Dhiraj: And the houseplants are also very attractive.

Sujata: They're my mother's specialty. Some of them are nearly twenty years old.

Dhiraj: Good heavens, how does she do it?

Sujata: She's got a really green thumb; plants seem to respond to her.

I wish I could play the piano like you!!!

Anita: I wish I could play the piano like you.

Disha: I'm sure you could if you tried. You should take some lessons.

Anita: I took some when I was younger but I was hopeless.

Disha: Why was that?

Anita: I found that I was tone-deaf, which really made it impossible.

Disha: Never mind, why don't you try learning the drums? Then being tone-deaf shouldn't matter.

I like the way you pan across the ruins!!!

Kunal: Your vacation video is really interesting.

Dinesh: Well, Mexico is a fascinating country.

Kunal: What are we looking at now?

Dinesh: These are the remains of a Mayan city.

Kunal: I like the way you pan across the ruins very slowly.

Dinesh: That helps you to see what a really large area they cover.

The Real goalie made a fantastic save!!!

Lokesh: Did you see the Barcelona-Real Madrid match on TV yesterday?

Kamal: Of course, what a game! Three goals each.

Lokesh: Who do you support?

Kamal: Real Madrid, because I'm a Beckham fan.

Lokesh: Barcelona should have won it with that great shot on goal in the last minute.

Kamal: Only they didn't because **the Real goalie made a fantastic save.**

She sight-reads really well!!!

Pooja: My elder sister is always in demand at family parties.

Asha: Why, is she a good singer?

Pooja: No, she plays the piano really well and she can play whatever music anyone puts in front of her.

Asha: I can play the piano, but I couldn't do that. How does she do it?

Pooja: She sight-reads really well.

Asha: I wish I could do that, it's a great skill.

She enjoys doing still lifes!!!

Richa: My sister started a new hobby a few months ago.

Seema: Really? Tell me more.

Richa: She's been learning to paint watercolours.

Seema: How interesting. What are her favourite subjects?

Richa: She likes painting landscapes best, but **she also enjoys doing still lifes.**

Seema: I envy her. I've tried to paint in the past, but I'm no good – I have no artistic talent.

They seem to have a lot in common!!!

Komal: Puja and Raja seem to be spending a lot of time together lately.

Preeti: Yes that's true. I've seen them at the swimming pool lately and at the cinema.

Komal: They go on regular bike rides together too.

Preeti: They seem to have a lot in common.

Komal: Yes, they clearly like the same things.

Preeti: I wonder if we'll be hearing wedding bells soon.

He's clearly over the moon about something!!!

Dhiraj: Have you seen Jeewan today?

Kabir: No, why?

Dhiraj: Well he's clearly over the moon about something.

Kabir: What about?

Dhiraj: He won't tell anybody, but I've never seen him looking so happy.

Kabir: He's a betting man, so perhaps he's won a lot of money on the horses.

What do you fancy?

Kabir: Let's eat out tonight. I don't feel like cooking.

Vikas: Well why not? What do you fancy?

Kabir: I think Japanese would make a nice change.

Vikas: Fine. How about that new place just off the market square?

Kabir: Good idea. I'll go and freshen up first.

Vikas: OK, in the meantime I'll phone to book a table.

He kept changing channels on the remote!!!

Kiran: My mother got really annoyed with my father yesterday evening.

Seema: Why, did he complain about her cooking?

Kiran: Oh no, she's a great cook. It was when they were watching television.

Seema: Don't tell me he fell asleep in front of the television and started snoring.

Kiran: No, he does that sometimes but this was because he kept changing channels on the remote.

Seema: All men do that, it's one of their most annoying habits.

My luggage went astray!!!

Nisha: I had a terrible time on my last trip to Europe.

Kartik: Why, what happened? Did you have an accident?

Nisha: No, my luggage went astray. When I arrived in Paris and went to collect my case from the baggage carousel, it never arrived.

Kartik: What happened to it? Had somebody collected it by mistake or stolen it?

Nisha: No, it had been sent on to London by mistake.

Kartik: Did you get it back.

Nisha: Yes I did, but it took two whole days. I was absolutely furious.

They've probably been held up by the traffic!!!

Somesh: You're not looking too cheerful.

Kamaljeet: Well, I arranged with Bob and Chetan to meet me here for a drink at seven o'clock. It's now a quarter to eight and neither of them has turned up.

Somesh: I wouldn't give up hope. **They've probably been held up by the traffic**. It's been very heavy for the past hour.

Kamaljeet: Even so, they should have turned up by now.

Somesh: Well, I'd give them another quarter of an hour or so.

Kamaljeet: OK, but after that I'm going home.

It really gets up my nose!!!

Suraj: It's been a pretty tight game so far, don't you think?

Kabir: Yes, neither side have looked like scoring a goal so far.

Suraj: Except that one time when our striker was almost through but was fouled by the fullback. The referee didn't see it.

Kabir: Yes, **it really gets up my nose** when something like that happens.

Suraj: Well, let's hope that the ref will be looking right way if that fullback tries playing dirty again.

Kabir: And then we'll get a penalty.

Stick at it!!!

Anil: Don't you find these rowing machines hard work?

Harish: I certainly do, but they're supposed to be.

Anil: How often do you come to the gym for a workout?

Harish: Three times a week at least if I can manage it.

Anil: No wonder you look so fit and trim.

Harish: Thanks. **Stick at it** and you can be the same.

Let's go for a spin!!!

Suresh: I'm feeling energetic today. **Let's go for a spin.**

Alam: OK. I need some exercise.

Suresh: Where shall we go?

Alam: Let's go around the lake, over the hill and come back through the wood.

Suresh: Fine, that's about 15 kilometres, enough for one day.

Alam: Don't forget your puncture outfit and crash helmet.

Go at steady pace!!!

Amit: Where are you going on the weekend?

Harish: I'm going hiking with some classmate.

Amit: Hiking? Isn't that rather strenuous?

Harish: Not if you **go at a steady pace** and take the occasional break.

Amit: Oh, that doesn't sound too bad.

Harish: Why don't you join us? You'll have a great time.

She just seems to have the knack!!!

Disha: I'm so envious of Lara's cooking.

Karishma: Me too, everything she does tastes perfect.

Disha: I tried some of her recipes myself, but they just don't seem to turn out right.

Karishma: You're not the only one, I tried to make her Black Forest cake the other day. It tasted all right but not half as good as Lara's.

Disha: How does she do it I wonder?

Karishma: She just seems to have the knack.

My battery must be low!!!

Girl: "Hello "?

AJ: "Hi it's me what's up baby? I'm sorry! Listen! I'm gonna be late tonight so don't stay up and wait for me OK?"

Girl: "Where are you?"

AJ: "Wait wait! Say that again?"

Girl: "Hello?"

AJ: "You're coming in and out I think my battery must be low. Listen! If you can hear me we're going to a place nearby, alright? Gotta go" (click)

Work like a charm!!!

Salesman: Lowest prices! Best quality! Hello, sir!

Buyer: Oh, hi. I'm just looking. I have a computer already.

Salesman: How long have you had it?

Buyer: Years. Works like a charm.

Salesman: Years? What a dinosaur! I can't believe you still use it.

Buyer: It's fine for writing letters and...

He is a good catch!!!

Kaushik: Guess who else is falling into the love trap.

Ahmed: It better not be Bobbie. I don't want to lose another friend to the death of love.

Kaushik: It's Marie. With the guy from New York..

Ahmed: No wonder! I saw her wearing a promise ring.

Kaushik: I encouraged her. I think he's a good catch.

Ahmed: It better not be just 'cuz he looks like Tom Cruise. Marriage is more than a fling with a movie-star look-alike.

Don't flatter yourself!!!

Kapil: What is that noise?

Harish: What noise?

Kapil: I hear a girl saying "Harry, honey. Please pick up the phone, you stud..."

Harish: Oh! That's my new cell phone. It must be my latest squeeze, Jane.

Kapil: Jane?

Harish: Yeah. She's totally into me. She calls me all the time.

Kapil: Don't flatter yourself!

In the air!!!

Harpreet: Jyotsna! Guess what. Leo proposed to me!

Jyotsna: Wow. Love is in the air. Did you accept?

Harpreet: Not yet. I have some doubts...like the age factor. I'm really robbing the cradle here.

Jyotsna: So he's eight years younger...he's mature for his age.

Harpreet: I'm worried about the cultural differences, too.

Jyotsna: You guys have the same interests and similar personalities and you have the same dreams.

Up to something!!!

Karina: Yeah, great. But who recorded these for you?

Vimal: My classmate, as a joke. It makes me sound like a womanizer.

Karina: Well, then let me record one for you.

Vimal: OK. Cool. Be sexy. Here. Go!

Karina: Hey, jerk! Answer the phone, you idiot!

Vimal: Hey! I should have known you were up to something.

In a row!!!

Ekta: The new year will be here before you know it.

Nisha: This year really went by fast.

Ekta: It seems every year goes by faster.

Nisha: I especially enjoy the new year, though.

Ekta: Why?

Nisha: We have three holidays **in a row**.

I'll tell you what!!!

Dhruv: Let's go to the movies in Prickly tomorrow.

Prakash: OK, where should we meet. Do you know where Lot 10 is? We went there together.

Dhruv: No, I don't remember. Let's meet somewhere outside Prickly.

Prakash: I'll tell you what — name the place and I'll pick you up.

Give it to me straight!!!

Boss: As you know Suraj, you are a highly-valued worker. However, the company has run into financial difficulty lately that are causing some unexpected repercussions.

Suraj: Like what! **Give it to me straight**.

Boss: I am afraid we have to lay you off.

Don't get me wrong!!!

Nisha: Don't get me wrong! I think Kaushal is a very nice person, but you have to admit he isn't very responsible.

Suraj: I think you are right, he has got a lot of growing up to do.

You can say that again!!!

Kapil: I think there is a sharp contrast between Americans and Chinese. For example, the Americans are very individualistic, while the Chinese are very group-oriented.

Yogesh: You can say that again. Chinese are very conscious of what other people think of them.

You are on the right track!!!

Suresh: I am trying to figure out who the murderer is in this story.

Ramesh: Who do you think it is!

Suresh: I think it's Mr. Ajay because he was in the house at the time of the murder.

Ramesh: No, but you **are on the right track**.

It's beyond me!!!

Amit: How long have you been in this country?

Yogesh: Two months.

Amit: Is he hard for you to study at an American college?

Yogesh: Yes, I find it very difficult. Especially when you can't follow the professor's lecture.

Amit: That's because you just arrived. Do you like biology?

Yogesh: No. **It's beyond me.**

Whatever you say!!!

Deepak: How about having dinner together after work?

Mukesh: Fine.

Deepak: Should we have Japanese or American food?

Mukesh: Whatever you say!

Deepak: There is a good steak house around the corner.

Mukesh: That's a good idea.

I am starving!!!

Kapil: I think we should get something to eat.

Tina: Are you hungry?

Kapil: Hungry? **I'm starving.**

Tina: There is an Italian restaurant near here.

Kapil: Is the food very hot?

Tina: It's kind of hot, but it's very tasty.

Rian check

Kapil: My brother and his family will be coming into town next week.

Kaushik: Is he the one who writes articles for the English Post?

Kapil: Right, why don't you come over next Sunday to meet him.

Kaushik: I'd love to but I can't. Can you give me a rian check!!!

Kapil: Sure, they'll be here for a week. So just let me know when you can come.

Kaushik: OK! I will be very interested in seeing him.

Brush up on!!!

Ashok: Do you have a driver's license?

Ashwani: No. I am going to take the test in a couple of weeks.

Ashok: Didn't you drive in your country?

Ashwani: Yes, but I have to brush up on my driving.

Ashok: And. You have to study the traffic rules too!

Ashwani: Yes, there is a lot of new things I must learn.

I am broke!!!

Dinesh: Are you going to Hawaii on your vacation?

Amit: Not this year.

Dinesh: Why not?

Amit: For a good reason, I am broke.

Dinesh: Oh! Come on.

Amit: Seriously, I am flat broke.

Out of the question!!!

Dinesh: I am going to look at new cars tomorrow.

Amit: I wish I could have one.

Dinesh: Why don't you come along?

Amit: I'd like to but I don't want to be tempted.

Dinesh: I am sure you could get a good deal.

Amit: No, buying a new car is out of the question for me right now.

Don't get me wrong!!!

Vimal: Bill is going to sing tonight.

Shilpa: Oh, no!

Vimal: Don't you like his singing?

Shilpa: It's not that. Don't get me wrong!!!

Vimal: What's the problem then?

Shilpa: He only knows one song.

I'll keep my fingers crossed!!!

Prashant: Please have a seat.

Pankaj: Thank you

Prashant: I'm Mr. Prashant. The personnel manager. What can I do for you.

Pankaj: I am looking for a position as a sales representative.

Prashant: We may have an opening next week. Please leave your resume, I will keep in touch with you.

Pankaj: Thanks. **I'll keep my fingers crossed.**

Does it ring a bell!!!

Seema: Guess who I met at the grocery store.

Lokesh: I can't imagine.

Seema: Do you remember Mr. Ritesh from our old neighbourhood.

Lokesh: That name **rings a bell**, but I can't place him.

Seema: He used to live in the building next to ours.

Lokesh: Oh yes, now I remember. He had dark hair and wore glasses.

Let's get to the point!!!

Supriya: Good afternoon Shalaj, isn't it a lovely day?

Shalaj: Yes, it is Supriya!

Supriya: It is the kind of day when you want to go outside.

Shalaj: Supriya, **let's get to the point**. Do you want the afternoon off?

Supriya: Yes, Bob.

Shalaj: Alright. As soon as you finish typing. You can go.

I tossed and turned all night!!!

Shalaj: Are you ill?

Reema: Not really! I am just tired.

Shalaj: Didn't you sleep well last night.

Reema: No, **I tossed and turned all night**.

Shalaj: I am sorry to hear that, I hope you sleep better tonight.

Reema: Thank you. I'm sure I will.

It's a piece of cake!!!

Harsh: What kind of Chinese food would you like to have.

Kaushik: I'd like to have spring rolls.

Harsh: Fine. By the way, do you know how to use chopsticks?

Kaushik: It's a piece of cake.

Harsh: How in the world did you learn to use them?

Kaushik: I was stationed in Taiwan for five years, you know.

Not that I know of !!!

Nisha: Is Mrs. Johnson joining us for dinner?

Seema: Not that I know of.

Nisha: I was hoping she would come with us.

Seema: Why?

Nisha: I would like her to try some of our traditional Indian foods.

Seema: That's very kind of you.

It is on the tip of my tongue!!!

Mukesh: Do you remember the restaurant we went to Friday.

Alok: Sure I do. It was the 'Silver Castle'.

Mukesh: No, we've never been to the 'Silver Castle'.

Alok: Maybe it was the Gold Coin.

Mukesh: No Gee. **It is on the tip of my tongue.**

Alok: Never mind. The food was terrible.

Chances are slim!!!

Rakhi: What are your chances of getting into Yale?

Ahmed: My chances are slim.

Rakhi: I hear those Ivy League Colleges are tough to get into.

Ahmed: I know. I'd have better chance at the state University.

Rakhi: Sure. It's not a bad school either.

Ahmed: I'd rather be a big fish in a small pond.

It doesn't make any difference!!!

Ashwani: Shall I pick you up at 5 or 6?

Suresh: It doesn't make any difference.

Ashwani: O.K, I will pick you up at 5.

Suresh: No problem!

Ashwani: Shall we play badminton or table tennis on Sunday?

Suresh: It doesn't make any difference.

It's better than nothing!!!

Somesh: Did you ask Mr. Davidson for a raise?

Kamal: Yes, I asked for 80 cents any hour more.

Somesh: Did you get it?

Kamal: No, I got 30 cents

Somesh: That's too bad.

Kamal: Oh, it is alright. It is better than nothing.

You can count on us!!!

Shikha: Sue, can you drive Jane and I to the doctor on Monday?

Sonal: I think so.

Shikha: We need a ride very badly, are you sure you will be able to help out?

Sonal: Sure. I will mark it on my calendar so I don't forget.

Shikha: Thanks you are a good friend.

Sonal: You can always count on me when you need help.

It is up to you!!!

Raju: Would you like to go out to dinner or to a movie?

Karan: Either one, it is up to you.

Raju: What would you prefer?

Karan: I really don't care, I just want to get out of the house.

Raju: Well, then how about dinner and a movie?

Karan: That's a great idea!

I couldn't help it!!!

Deepak: I am upset. Somebody told my boss I have a part-time job.

Sumit: And he doesn't like that?

Deepak: No, he doesn't. He thinks that I am too tired to work.

Sumit: I am sorry. I have to admit I told him.

Deepak: You told him? Why?

Sumit: I couldn't help it. He asked me point-blank.

Reducing and enlarging facility!!!

Kamal: I have to photocopy these two documents. I need a copy of this one smaller than the original, and of the other larger.

Rishi: Well you'll need to use the reducing and enlarging facility on the photocopier.

Kamal: The copy of this one should be half the size of the original, and the other twice the size.

Rishi: Lift the lid and put the first document on the glass face down, then press the button marked 200% and you'll get a copy twice the size of the original.

Kamal: OK. What about the other one?

Rishi: When you've copied the first one, put the other one face down on the glass, press the button marked 50% and you'll get a half-size copy.

That's really wasteful!!!

Raj: Look at all the waste paper in the waste bin next to the photocopier.

Rishi: There is rather a lot but it's the same with all the photocopier.

Raj: What do they do with all that waste paper?

Rishi: As far as I know they just throw it out as trash.

Raj: That's really wasteful. There's a better way of dealing with it than that.

Rishi: Well we should try to recycle all our waste paper. That would save the company a lot of money and help the environment.

It's very temperamental!!!

Ram: Why has the photocopier stopped?

Rajesh: Oh, it's probably because the paper has jammed. You'll have to open the door and look inside the machine to check.

Ram: Oh yes, I can see where a sheet of paper has got stuck.

Rajesh: You need to follow the instructions printed inside the door to remove it and restart the machine.

Ram: That wasn't too difficult. Well, I'll restart the machine and hope for the best.

Rajesh: You'll need a lot of hope for that machine. **It's very temperamental** and really needs replacing.

It doesn't collate!!!

Harish: I've got this 32-page report and I need to make 40 copies.

Raju: Well you can't do that on our photocopier.

Harish: Why not? There's nothing wrong with it, is there?

Raju: No, but **it's a basic model and doesn't collate**.

Harish: Where can I find a photocopier which does?

Raju: Try the Project Department. They're always producing reports so I'm sure they must have a machine that does the job.

Time for elevenses!!!

Rahul: I haven't started work so early in weeks.

Shyam: Yes, it's only a quarter to ten and we've been at it for almost four hours.

Rahul: Time for elevenses before we die of hunger and thirst.

Shyam: Great idea. I'll pop out and get some doughnuts.

Rahul: And I'll put the kettle on.

Shyam: Oh yes, I'm just dying for a cup of tea.

A light supper wouldn't do us any harm!!!

Bobby: It's some time since we've eaten. I'm quite hungry, what about you?

Gyan: I'm a bit peckish too, but it's quite late and we don't want anything too heavy before we go to bed.

Bobby: What do you suggest?

Gyan: Well, **a little light supper wouldn't do us any harm**!

Bobby: Such as?

Gyan: I could make a cheese and potato salad.

Bobby: That'll do nicely.

We'll be able to dine alfresco!!!

Sohail: Where shall we eat after the show?

Raj: What about that restaurant down by the river?

Sohail: Do you mean the one with peacocks running around the garden?

Raj: That's the one. It's very traditional and I just love the atmosphere.

Sohail: And it's such a warm and pleasant evening that we'll be able to dine alfresco on the riverside terrace.

Raj: Yes, that would be lovely. And with the sky so clear we'll be dining by moonlight. How romantic!

Take me back!!!

Rohan: This takes me back, I haven't been to the seaside since I was a child.

Rohit: I haven't been for ages either.

Rohan: Tell you what, let's go on the pier and get some cotton candy.

Rohit: But that's for kids and it's pure sugar; it'll ruin your figure.

Rohan: I don't care, it was one of my favorite things to have when we came to the seaside.

Rohit: Well, if you're going to relive your childhood, I'm going to have to do the same.

A3-sized copies!!!

Rajesh: This document is A3 size and I've got to make three A3-sized copies.

Vicky: That's no problem on this photocopier as it's got an A3 paper tray.

Rajesh: I've put the document face down on the glass, what do I do next?

Vicky: Open the door and check that there's paper in the A3 paper tray.

Rajesh: Yes, it's almost full.

Vicky: Close the door, select the A3 paper tray on the control panel and then press the green button to start copying.

Put the document face down!!!

Ginny: I want to make some A4 copies but I've never used a photocopier before. Could you please help me?

Harsh: Of course. First of all lift the lid and put the document you want to copy face down on the glass.

Ginny: OK. What do I do now?

Harsh: Make sure that it's straight and within the A4 lines marked on the glass. Then lower the lid.

Ginny: There, done that. Now what?

Harsh: Enter the number of copies you want using these button and then press the big green button to start.

Ginny: That's a breeze!

Stock up on that!!!

Rakesh: I've almost finished the preparations for our expedition.

Rohit: Where are you planning to go?

Rakesh: We're going to spend two weeks in northern Norway.

Rohit: That's pretty tough country. You'll need a lot of energy.

Rakesh: That's why we're taking lots of Kendal mint cake.

Rohit: I'm not surprised. A lot of expeditions stock up on that before they go.

Double-sided printing!!!

Sagar: Have you seen the e-mail from the supplies department?

Shankar: No, I haven't. What does it say?

Sagar: It says that in future when photocopying we should use **double-sided printing** wherever possible.

Shankar: Well I suppose only using one side of the paper is wasteful.

Sagar: Doing this should cut out paper bill by 50 percent.

Shankar: Yes. And think of all the trees we'll save by using double-sided.

Go in for a pie and a pint!!!

Rohit: Punting's thirsty work and it's almost one o'clock.

Sumit: Talk about thirsty, I'm pretty hungry as well.

Rohit: Do you see what I see?

Sumit: You mean that pub just on the next bend in the river?

Rohit: Right first time. Are you thinking what I'm thinking?

Sumit: Yes, let's tie up there and **go in for a pie and a pint**.

Let the teapot stand!!!

Sunny: Teach me how to make a pot of tea.

Pritam: Well, first of all you need a china teapot. Tea doesn't taste so good from a metal one.

Sunny: What next?

Pritam: Rinse out the teapot with very hot water to make it hot.

Sunny: Then boil the kettle?

Pritam: That's right. Then put two or three teaspoons of tea into the teapot, take the kettle to the pot and pour the boiling water over the tea.

Sunny: Can you drink it straight away?

Pritam: No, you have to **let the teapot stand** for a few minutes and then the tea will be ready to drink.

You need to increase the contrast!!!

Raj: My copies have started coming out a bit faint.

Suraj: Let me have a look. Yes they should be a bit darker than that.

Raj: How can I do that on this machine?

Suraj: You need to increase the contrast by pressing this button here. You've got a choice of five levels. Try the third one. You'll need to press the button three times.

Raj: The copies look fine now, just what the doctor ordered. Thanks a lot.

Suraj: Don't mention it.

The copies are faint!!!

Tarun: That's annoying. **The copies are suddenly coming out very faint.**

Suraj: Let's have a look. Yes, you can hardly read the text.

Tarun: What should I do?

Suraj: Well you could try taking out the toner cartridge, giving it a good shake, and putting it back.

Tarun: It worked. The copies are much clearer. Thanks a lot.

Suraj: No problem. That trick will work a couple of times. After that, the machine will need a new toner cartridge.

Run out of!!!

Shikha: Oh no! It's always the same.

Kamaljeet: What's the matter?

Shikha: The photocopier's **run out of** paper.

Kamaljeet: Have you looked in the store cupboard for more?

Shikha: Yes, of course. But that's out of paper as well.

Kamaljeet: That's really bad luck. If your job's really urgent, I would go to the copy bureau across the street.

Shikha: Thanks. It is and I will.

Have a go at you!!!

Foreigner: That man at the bar got really annoyed with me just now.

Friend: Yes, I could see him having a go at you. What was the reason?

Foreigner: I wanted to get drinks for us and he said I had jumped the queue. But people weren't standing in line at the bar.

Friend: That's true, but there actually was still a queue in the sense that the rule is "first come, first served" and he must have been at the bar before you.

Foreigner: Where I come from, it's every man for himself.

Friend: But not here I'm afraid, so it's best to follow the local rule if you want to avoid such unpleasantness.

You must be starving!!!

Bobby: You've been working on that file for almost five hours without a break. You must be starving.

Rishi: Yes, I am a bit peckish, especially as I didn't have anything for breakfast.

Bobby: Well the only place you can get food around here at this time of day is the "Dog and Duck" across the road.

Rishi: What's the food like there?

Bobby: It's not bad. They don't do hot food but their ploughman's lunch is really tasty. The bread and cheese are always really fresh and they make their own pickle.

Rishi: Sounds good. I'll shoot over straight away. Care to join me?

I love your tea cozy!!!

Rahul: May I pour you another cup of tea?

Disha: Thank you, that's very kind. I must say I love your tea cozy. The design is very attractive.

Rahul: I'm glad you like it. It's one of many my mother made.

Disha: Well, she was clearly very skilled with the needle.

Rahul: Yes, she was; needlework was her favourite hobby.

What beautiful China!!!

Nidhi: Thank you for inviting me to tea, it's really good of you.

Neha: Not at all, we're delighted to have you. May I pour you a cup of tea?

Nidhi: Oh, yes, thank you very much. What beautiful China!

Neha: I'm glad you like it. This is part of tea service which my grandmother left me. I was her only granddaughter.

Nidhi: It's all so artistically decorated.

Neha: It is very fine work and genuine Chinese porcelain.

Nidhi: No doubt that's why your tea tastes so good.

Neha: Thank you. They do say that tea always tastes better from real porcelain.

What's clotted cream?

Geeta: Now we're in the countryside, there's one thing we just mustn't miss.

Raj: What's that, drinking the local cider?

Geeta: No, it's having a real cream tea.

Raj: What's so special about that?

Geeta: Well, it's having real clotted cream on your scones with home-made strawberry jam to go with your tea.

Raj: What's clotted cream?

Geeta: It's thickest and most delicious cream there is.

Just what the doctor ordered!!!

Asha: I'm dying for a cup of tea and I'm also a bit peckish.

Raj: What about that place over there. "Ye Olde Tea Shoppe"?

Asha: Just what the doctor ordered. It's almost 4 o'clock, let's go in and have afternoon tea.

Raj: (To waitress) A pot of tea for two please.

Asha: And I'd like some salmon sandwiches and a cream cake

Raj: Watch your figure there. I think I'll just have some toast with strawberry jam.

Time for high tea!!!

Karishma: It's 4 o'clock, **time for high tea**.

Radha: So early? Six o'clock or thereabouts is high tea time.

Karishma: What? Tea, sandwiches and cakes at 6 o'clock? That's a surely far too late.

Radha: No, no. I think you're mixing up high tea and afternoon tea.

Karishma: Aren't they the same?

Radha: No, not at all. Afternoon tea means tea, perhaps sandwiches and definitely cakes around 4.

Karishma: What's high tea, then?

Radha: That's a proper meal, often with meat or fish, but also of course with tea to drink.

He stood us all a round of drinks!!!

Rohan: You missed a treat last night.

Rajesh: Why, what happened?

Rohan: Well, Benny came into our local, told us that he'd just played a round of golf and scored a hole in one at the 18th.

Rajesh: So what? Everyone gets lucky now and again.

Rohan: Ah, but **he stood us all a round of drinks.**

Rajesh: Now that's what I call a real sportsman.

Is this just a one-off?

Ronit: You must come to my local tomorrow evening.

Raju: Why, what's on?

Ronit: It's darts night. Our pub's team is playing against the team from the "Lord Nelson" across the park. I'm in the team and we need all the support we can get.

Raju: Is this just a one-off?

Ronit: Oh no. We're in a league of 20 pub teams and there's a game every week.

Raju: Where does your team stand?

Ronit: We're second in the league and could go top if we beat the "Lord Nelson" tomorrow.

Let's go to my local!!!

Ashok: Well, we've got through a pile of work and it's past opening time. Let's go for a pint.

Kamal: Good idea, where shall we go?

Ashok: Let's go to my local, it's just around the corner.

Kamal: I think I must have passed it on the way here. Is it the "Rose and Crown"?

Ashok: That's it. It's a really old place with lots of atmosphere.

Kamal: Great stuff, lead on MacDuff.

What's it for?

Seema: What's that above the bar? It looks like a long glass trumpet with a glass bulb at the end.

Somesh: It's a yard of ale, that's to say it's a bit less than a meter long.

Seema: What's it for?

Somesh: It's for a traditional beer-drinking competition.

Seema: Who wins?

Somesh: The person who can drink a pint of beer from it fastest without spilling a drop. It's very difficult. The record in this pub is 9 seconds.

You were really tipsy!!!

Murli: Lulu's hen party last night was really wild, wasn't it?

Mohit: Yes, look at the horrible bags under our eyes.

Murli: I really had a bit too much to drink. No wonder I feel so rough.

Mohit: Yes, you were really tipsy by the end.

Murli: I think I'd better keep off alcohol for a bit.

Mohit: Good idea, I think I'll do the same. Our systems need to recover.

It showed documentaries!!!

Raj: Have you seen the movie Fahrenheit 9/11?

Tony: No, what is it, a science fiction adventure?

Raj: No it's a documentary about American politics after the World Trade Center tragedy in September 2001.

Tony: Did you see it on television?

Raj: No, at our local movie theater. It's been on all this week.

Tony: I didn't know it showed documentaries.

Raj: It doesn't normally, but there has been huge demand to see this one.

Draught or bottled?

Dhiraj: I've worked up a bit of a thirst after all that walking and this looks like a really nice pub. Shall we go in?

Mohit: Why not? We could do with a rest.

Dhiraj: (At the bar) Now what can I get you?

Mohit: I'd like a half of lager please.

Dhiraj: Draught or bottled?

Mohit: Bottled please. I prefer German beer and they don't seem to have any on draught.

Some love interest!!!

Kiran: I didn't really enjoy that movie at all.

Suman: Why not? I thought it was really exciting with lots of action.

Kiran: Typical man, that's just what you would like.

Suman: Well what would you have wanted?

Kiran: Some love interest, not just car chases and fights.

Suman: Typical female, you're only interested in romance.

The score was fantastic!!!

Priyanka: I haven't enjoyed a movie so much in years.

Rohan: Yes, it really was something special.

Priyanka: It had a great story and the acting was absolutely fantastic.

Rohan: **The score was fantastic** too. It really added to the action.

Priyanka: Yes it was really good music and it had such a haunting theme.

Rohan: If they bring it out on CD, I'll be the first to buy it.

A movie crew was shooting on location!!!

Karthik: You'll never guess what was going on in our town last week.

Rajesh: Go on, surprise me.

Karthik: **A movie crew was shooting on location** in the town square.

Rajesh: Really? Why did they choose your town?

Karthik: Because the square's full of old buildings which were a perfect background for the kind of historical movie they were making.

Rajesh: I'd love to have been there. I've never seen a movie crew in action before.

Change hands!!!

Vandana: This pub's just **changed hands** you know.

Payal: Is that right? Who's got it now?

Vandana: The publican wanted to retire so he sold it to one of the big breweries.

Payal: (Rings bell). Last orders, please!

Vandana: Oh no, the saddest words a man will ever hear. One more before we go?

Payal: Yes please, but be careful you don't get trampled in the rush.

I had to rely on the subtitles!!!

Kapil: I've just seen the latest movie from China.

Rohit: Good?

Kapil: Oh yes. It was about a family who lived in the late Qing dynasty.

Rohit: I know you're learning Chinese. Did you understand everything?

Kapil: No, not really. They spoke too fast for me to catch much, so **I had to rely on the subtitles**.

Rohit: Yes, they're always very helpful when you're watching a foreign-language movie.

Violence is good box office!!!

Geeta: That was a really violent movie.

Kapil: It certainly was. There seemed to be one killing about every ten minutes.

Geeta: I know. I began to get a bit sick of it long before the end.

Kapil: Why are so many movies so full of violence?

Geeta: It's because **violence is good box office** I suppose.

Kapil: You must be right. Well the next movie I go to see will be romantic comedy.

Looking back on his life in flashback!!!

Gopal: I've just seen a really interesting foreign movie.

Rohit: Really? Where was it made?

Gopal: In Iran. I didn't even know it had a movie industry.

Rohit: Neither did I. What was it about?

Gopal: It was about an old man on his deathbed **looking back on his life in flashback**.

Rohit: Sounds a bit depressing.

Gopal: Not at all, he had had a very exciting life.

Are you a regular?

Stranger 1: Ah, great taste! They certainly know how to keep beer here.

Stranger 2: Yes, the publican's very fussy about how it's stored and at what temperature.

Stranger 1: And the variety of beers seems to be much greater than in your average pub.

Stranger 2: That's true. He's very keen on beers from small, independent breweries and we've got quite a few around here.

Stranger 1: Are you a regular?

Stranger 2: Oh yes, I've been coming here once or twice a week for years. Can't keep me away.

There'll be just a few trailers!!!

Prakas'ı: Thank goodness the ads are over. They go on for far too long.

Raj: Yes, there'll be just a few trailers and then the movie will start.

Prakash: I don't mind trailers, at least they're not trying to sell you anything.

Raj: Of course, they are, they're trying to sell you the latest movies.

Prakash: Well, I suppose so, but they're a lot more exciting than the ads.

Raj: If you ask me, they're sometimes a lot more exciting than the movies themselves.

He's down the pub!!!

Raja: Where's Paul? I've been looking for him everywhere.

Tony: I don't know, haven't seen him all day.

Raja: What's the time?

Tony: It's just gone 7.

Raja: Well, what a silly question!

Tony: What do you mean?

Raja: Well **he's down the pub** of course. He's there every night.

Fancy another?

Jyoti: Have you enjoyed the evening?

Sujata: Oh yes, you've taken me to places I never knew existed.

Jyoti: Well you're pretty new here and I've been working in this area for almost five years, so I know most of the good places by now.

Sujata: And this is one of the nicest pubs I've been in.

Jyoti: It is very attractive. **Fancy another?**

Sujata: I'd better not. It's time to go and I really need my beauty sleep as I've got to get up very early in the morning.

He only drinks shorts!!!

Kamaljeet: I was out on the town with Ollie last night.

Rajesh: Where did you go?

Kamaljeet: Oh, lots of places, but we ended up in the "Queen's Head".

Rajesh: Have a good time?

Kamaljeet: Oh sure, but Ollie's a rather expensive drinking companion.

Rajesh: Why's that?

Kamaljeet: **He only drinks shorts** and he can certainly put them away.

It's my round!!!

Dhruv: Fantastic shot.

Suresh: Yes, he really did bend it like Beckham.

Dhruv: This is a great pub for football, they've got such a big screen.

Suresh: Yes, it's almost like actually being at the match.

Dhruv: Would you like another drink?

Suresh: I certainly could, but stay put, **it's my round**.

They hold a referendum!!!

Abhishek: I've been working in Switzerland for some time now and I find their political system very interesting.

Kunal: Isn't it very similar to ours?

Abhishek: Not really, there is much more direct democracy there.

Kunal: How does it work?

Abhishek: If there is an important question to be decided, at national or local level, **they hold a referendum** so that the people can decide for themselves.

Kunal: That's quite different from our representative system.

Won by a landslide!!!

Ravi: You look pretty depressed, what's the matter?

Harsh: I've just come from our party's headquarters. Everyone there feels the same.

Ravi: You must have lost the election then?

Harsh: We did, and after all that hard work, canvassing for days on end.

Ravi: Is it really that bad?

Harsh: It is. The other side **won by a landslide**. It's our worst defeat in ten years.

A real cliff-hanger!!!

Raj: This is one of the closest elections I can remember.

Akash: Yes, that's true whichever part of the country you look at.

Raj: In the west, the candidates have equal support in the polls.

Akash: And in the rest of the country there is very little to separate them.

Raj: This election is clearly going to be **a real cliff-hanger**.

Akash: Yes, we won't know the result until all the votes have been counted.

Where are you off to!!!

Ashok: Where are you off to in such a hurry?

Kabir: I'm just off to the movie theater to see the latest Nicole Kidman movie.

Ashok: I've seen it, it's really good. Have you got a ticket?

Kabir: No, I'll buy one at the box office.

Ashok: You could have saved yourself a lot of time by buying it on the internet.

Kabir: I didn't know you could do that. You must show me how to do it.

I got them through my friend!!!

Disha: You're looking very pleased with yourself? How come?

Somesh: Look what I've got - two tickets for the premiere of the latest Tom Cruise movie and the reception afterwards.

Disha: Wow! How did you get them?

Somesh: I got them through my friend. His brother's in the movie distribution business.

Disha: Are they good seats?

Somesh: I'll say. They're in the front row of the balcony, right in the middle.

I've still got a long way to go!!!

Tony: Did you enjoy our round of golf?

Ramesh: I certainly did. It's the first time I've managed to break 75 for the course.

Tony: That's true, so well done! It shows how much you've improved.

Ramesh: Perhaps, but **I've still got a long way to go** before I can be really satisfied with my game.

Tony: What aspect of your game do you think needs improving most?

Ramesh: Oh, without doubt my short game. I seem to drive reasonably well but I tend to drop shots around the green.

The camera zoomed in on the girl's face!!!

Radha: I've just seen an absolutely wonderful movie, so romantic.

Sujata: What was it about?

Radha: It was a very sad love story.

Sujata: How did it end?

Radha: The camera zoomed in on the girl's face as her lover was being forced to leave her, probably forever. Tears were just beginning to roll down her cheeks.

Sujata: Too gloomy for me I'm afraid. I like comedies.

My head is spinning now.

Reema: You look tired. Didn't you get enough sleep last night?

Raj: No. I had a bunch of my friends over and we partied until the wee hours.

Reema: No wonder you look so bad!

Raj: I guess I just can't take late nights like I used to. My head is spinning and I have a migraine.

Reema: I think you need to go home and take a rest.

Raj: I wish I could. But I don't think I can keep my eyes open long enough to drive home.

Reema: Don't worry. I'll give you a ride home. But next time, watch the partying, OK?

Even goose bumps have goose bumps.

Neha: Geez! Your room is like an ice-box!

Ashok: No, it's not! It's just comfortable.

Neha: Yeah, if you're a penguin. Just look at me! Even my goose bumps have goose bumps!

Ashok: Get outta here! I think you're exaggerating!

Neha: No, I'm not? Where's the thermostat?

Ashok: By the door, on the wall.

Neha: No wonder I'm cold! This thing is set at 65?!

Ashok: Like I said -- perfect!

Neha: If you live in Alaska. By the way, where's the shovel?

Ashok: Why do you need a shovel?

Neha: So I can dig us out when it starts snowing in here.

No wonder you're livid!

Ekta: You look so angry. What happened?

Tony: Nothing. I'd rather not talk about it. Just don't ask.

Ekta: Come on. I think you need to let off some steam. Besides, you shouldn't keep your feelings pent up. They'll eat you alive. So, talk to me.

Tony: All right. This morning I took my car to the garage to have them check the air-conditioner. They only gave it a once-over, refilled it with some Freon, and charged me 300 bucks!

Ekta: No wonder you're livid. I'd be mad, too if someone ripped me off like that.

Tony: Yeah. AND they were rude. They said I didn't know anything about cars, which I don't, but they didn't have to be so blunt!

Ekta: Sounds like you got a raw deal! Maybe you should file a complaint with the Consumer Protection Forum

Her skin looks so baby smooth!

Ashok: She's really pretty, isn't she? Her skin looks so baby smooth!

Kim: Well, it's just that she puts lots of make-up on her face. Actually, natural beauty comes from within.

Ashok: Ah, I can smell jealousy in the air!

Kim: She has nothing that deserves my jealousy. I don't have to put things on my face and I still look pretty. Don't you think so?

Ashok: Yeah, right! But what did you put on your face last night, those little greenish things?

Kim: They're cucumbers. They're natural skin soothers, natural healers of the skin. Haven't you heard them say on TV that...erh...they soften the skin, wipe out the roughness, counter irritation, and build strength and resilience?

Ashok: Yeah, yeah, yeah! They wipe out tight, tired feelings and remove lines and age signs. Blah, blah, blah, blah, blah! See I can even recite it.

Kim: That's right! You've learned a lot, haven't you?

It wasn't just any snore!

Kiran: Rakhi you look bushed. Didn't you get a good night's sleep?

Rakhi: Kiran. Mohan kept me awake all last night.

Kiran: Oh!?

Rakhi: I don't know why. Mohan rarely snores, but last night he really started sawing some logs! And it wasn't just any snore. It was more like a herd of elephants running through the room!

Kiran: My grandpa used to do the same thing. Sometimes he would even wake himself up. He snored so loud! I always thought it was funny.

Rakhi: Well, I'm certainly not laughing about Mohan. I don't think I can take another night like that again.

Kiran: Have you considered buying some earplugs?

Rakhi: You bet! In fact, I'm going to buy some at lunch!

The razor burn is really irritating.

Simi: Oh, what happened to your face, Raj? It looks like a heat rash.

Raj: It's a razor burn. I cut myself when I shaved this morning. The burns and cuts are really irritating.

Simi: I know how you feel. Maybe you shouldn't have grown a long, long beard.

Raj: Well, I thought it would be fun and would make me look more mature and sophisticated.

Simi: Yeah, my Mature man!

Raj: Any advice?

Simi: Maybe you could shave in the shower. The steam really helps soften your beard and moustache.

Raj: Hm, sounds like a good idea.

Simi: And you should avoid pressing too hard or tugging on your skin while shaving.

Raj: I guess I've been stretching it too often when I shave.

Simi: Hm. I would also suggest you try this cream I have. Use it on the affected area. It really helps moisturize your skin and lessen irritations

He flared up at me!

Sheena: You look like you're fuming. What's going on?

Rajiv: The boss is being unreasonable! He flared up at me, making a mountain out of molehill!

Sheena: What's the "molehill" he made a mountain out of?

Rajiv: I only made a few more copies, and I didn't think it was any big deal, but he blew up at me!

Sheena: Well, he has been under a lot of pressure recently. The company has been losing money and he's been a little bit depressed.

Rajiv: Well, I know he has the blues, but it doesn't mean he can vent his anger on me.

We should have a heart-to-heart chat!

Ashok: So, how is your new roommate?

Lokesh: She really turns me off.

Ashok: What happened?

Lokesh: She's always making loud noises at midnight and when I remind her, she always makes rude remarks.

Ashok: Why don't you have a heart to heart chat with her?

Lokesh: I tried, but it didn't work.

Ashok: But how many times did you try?

Lokesh: At least three times. I guess I'm going to complain to the manager. I hope she can be evicted.

What's wrong with the drain?

Radha: So, what's wrong with the drain?

Tina: It's clogged and the water won't go down.

Radha: Let me take a look. You know why? It's clogged with hair. No wonder the water won't go down.

Tina: Well, I guess the people who lived here before didn't clean the bathtub.

Radha: You're darn right!

Tina: But what should I do now?

Radha: Don't worry. I've got some acid here. It'll help dissolve the hair down there.

Tina: Erh! It stinks! Peehew!

Radha: Now you know you'll have to clean your bathtub every time after you use it.

I'm on a diet to lose weight!

Raj: Would you like to have some ice-cream? I've got a variety of flavors for you to choose from. I've got strawberry, peach, chocolate, chocolate chip, chocolate brownie, coffee, vanilla, rocky road, butter pecan, and praline.

Simi: Wow! What choices you have! I wish I could, but I just can't. I'm on a diet to lose weight.

Raj: Come on, it's just a bite. It doesn't really hurt to have just a bite.

Simi: I'd better not. Please don't tempt me. Please!

Raj: Gee! You are really strong-willed.

Simi: You're darn right. I'm not so easily coaxed into doing something that I think is wrong.

Raj: Well, I'd better not tempt you. Otherwise, if I give you a piece of cake, you might ask for a glass of milk.

I'd like to reserve a table for dinner.

Hostess: Pompas. How may I help you?

Ashwani: Yes. I'd like to reserve a table for dinner.

Hostess: How large a group are you expecting?

Ashwani: Six couples.

Hostess: Would you like to reserve a private dinning room?

Ashwani: That sounds like a good idea.

Hostess: All right. May I have your name, sir?

Ashwani: My name is Ashwani.

Hostess: What time will you be arriving?

Ashwani: Around 7:30 PM.

Hostess: All right, Mr. Ashwani. We have reserved a private dinning room for you at 7:30 PM. Thanks for calling Pompas.

Ashwani: Thank you very much.

I think school is giving me hives!

Anita: Hey, Reema. How's it going?

Reema: Not too great. I'm really stressed out.

Anita: Oh?

Reema: Yeah, I think school is giving me hives. See?

Anita: Oh, my gosh! Your arm is full of bumps!

Reema: And that's not the worst of it. You should see the bumps on my legs.

Anita: What did the doctor say?

Reema: He said to relax and take a break, but we both know I don't have any time for relaxing.

Anita: Yeah, but if you don't, it's only going to get worse.

Reema: I know, I know.... Maybe I can relax after this paper.

Anita: I sure hope so.

It knocks out bacteria and stops inflammation.

Amit: My toes feel very itchy. It's really irritating. I don't know what's happening.

Anita: Let me take a look. Ah-huh, I think you have athlete's foot.

Amit: What are you talking about? I'm not an athlete!

Anita: Come on, Amit, stop joking. You'd better take care of it before it gets worse. Imagine you have pus gushing out and rashes all over your legs....

Amit: Stop it, "Dr." Anita.

Anita: OK, OK. I guess I've got some cream for it. It really fixes skin in trouble. It's really a help for irritations and blemishes.

Amit: Is it this one?

Anita: Not really. That one is for heat burns.

Amit: Have you had athlete's foot before?

Anita: Yeah. It was a very bad experience. You know, if you don't keep your feet dry and clean, the fungus will grow and spread out quickly.

Amit: So my case isn't that bad, huh?

Anita: You're lucky. Yeah, here it is. Now apply it to the affected areas. This cream is very effective in clearing out bacteria and stopping inflammation from developing.

I think I'm running a temperature!

Dinesh: I think I'm running a temperature. My head is spinning, my mouth feels like cotton, and I have a scratchy throat.

Leena: Let me see. Hmm, you'd better stay at home today. And don't work on the computer! Staying up late with that thing has obviously played havoc with your health.

Dinesh: I can't help it. I guess I'm addicted to the Internet.

Leena: If you want to keep yourself in good shape, you'd better quit surfing the Net deep into the night. I don't want you kicking the bucket!

Don't you have air-conditioning in your apartment?

Suman: Don't you have air-conditioning in your apartment? It's sweltering here!

Richa: Well, there's air-conditioning. Did you see that window air-conditioner there? The problem is that the window unit is not powerful enough.

Suman: I guess not, huh.

Richa: Well, I'm going to move out anyway. The new apartment has central air-conditioning.

Suman: You should've moved out long, long ago.

Richa: Well, I had to wait until the lease expired. So....

Suman: So how can you stand the heat?

Richa: Well, I open the windows and...and I've got an electric fan here. It helps a little.

■

24 Common Mistakes

It is important for English speaking learners to have a look at some of the mistakes commonly made even by frequent readers and writers of English language. Given here are wrong sentences as well as their correct forms. Pay attention to the mistakes to avoid them while bring English language into daily usage.

Wrong: It's seven twenty o'clock.

Correct: It's seven twenty.

****

Wrong: Your coat is broken.

Correct: Your coat is torn.

****

Wrong: The last bus leaves at eleven o'clock. It's about eleven now, Hurry up!

Correct: The last bus leaves at eleven o'clock. It's nearly (almost) eleven now, Hurry up!

****

Wrong: It was still bright outside.

Correct: It was still light outside.

Wrong: I recommend you to take a long vacation.

Correct: I recommend that you take a long vacation.

****

Wrong: Come to here.

Correct: Come here.

****

Wrong: Common students in US don't wear a uniform.

Correct: The average students in US don't wear a uniform.

****

Wrong: Who cooked this salad?

Correct: Who made this salad?

****

Wrong: Different from me, she is proficient in English.

Correct: Unlike me, she is proficient in English.

****

Wrong: Little children are difficult to understand that.

Correct: It is difficult for children to understand that.

****

Wrong: Don't step on the grass.

Correct: Keep off the grass.

****

Wrong: Joseph did not go to the concert last week, I did not go too.

Correct: Joseph did not go to the concert last week, I did not go either.

Wrong: We have been waiting for half an hour. She has still not come.

Correct: We have been waiting for half an hour. She has not come yet.

****

Wrong: The hinges of the door had rusted. We had to push hardly to open it.

Correct: The hinges of the door had rusted. We had to push hard to open it.

****

Wrong: I get my salary twice a month.

Correct: I get paid twice a month..

****

Wrong: Would you like a drink?

Correct: Would you like something to drink?

****

Wrong: Let me examine your pulse.

Correct: Let me feel your pulse.

****

Wrong: I have no exercise talent.

Correct: I am not athletic.

****

Wrong: Don't expect me too much.

Correct: Don't expect too much from (of) me.

Wrong: This book deserves to read several times.

Correct: This book deserves to be read several times.

****

Wrong: I like red tea.

Correct: I like black tea.

****

Wrong: History repeats.

Correct: History repeats itself.

****

Wrong: I make a rule of going to bed early and get up early.

Correct: I make a rule to keep early hours.

****

Wrong: I went to the sea.

Correct: I went to the beach.

****

Wrong: I know his face.

Correct: I know him by sight.

****

Wrong: I forget my hat in the house.

Correct: I left my hat in the house.

****

Wrong: If you determine to make the grade in the entrance examination, you must work extra hard.

Correct: If you are determined to make the grade in the entrance examination, you must work extra hard.

Wrong: I have a free time.

Correct: I am free.

****

Wrong: Please handle this gold watch carefully. It worths more than ten thousand rupees.

Correct: Please handle this gold watch carefully. It is worth more than ten thousand rupees.

****

Wrong: I ran into Maria yesterday morning. She looked healthily.

Correct: I ran into Maria yesterday morning. She looked healthy.

****

Wrong: I am the only son in the family. I have not brothers.

Correct: I am the only son in the family. I have no brothers.

****

Wrong: My borther has been busy in preparing for his final examination.

Correct: My brother has been busy preparing for his final examination.

****

Wrong: Susan didn't make a fault anyway.

Correct: Susan didn't make a mistake anyway.

****

Wrong: Would you mind posting this letter for me? Yes, certainly.

Correct: Would you mind mailing this letter for me? Of course not. OR (Not at all)

Wrong: He becomes better.

Correct: He got better.

****

Wrong: We'll have a hearing test tomorrow.

Correct: We'll have a listening test tomorrow.

****

Wrong: I'll go there at three.

Correct: I'll be there at three.

****

Wrong: I am going back my home.

Correct: I am going home.

****

Wrong: His temperature went down.

Correct: His temperature came down.

****

Wrong: I like green colour.

Correct: I like green.

****

Wrong: Today's newspapers has his articles on Talivan.

Correct: Today's newspapers carries his articles on Talivan.

****

Wrong: You'll have a cold if you sleep with your window open.

Correct: You'll catch a cold if you sleep with your window open.

Wrong: Give me money, if you have.

Correct: Give me money, if you have any.

****

Wrong: Somebody's knocking on the door. Go and see who he is.

Correct: Somebody's knocking on the door. Go and see who it is.

****

Wrong: The head office is in Jaipur.

Correct: The main office is in Jaipur.

****

Wrong: He cannot read and write.

Correct: He cannot read or write.

****

Wrong: Where is here.

Correct: Where are we.

****

Wrong: How heavy are you?

Correct: How much do you weigh?

****

Wrong: He was talking in a high voice.

Correct: He was talking loud.

****

Wrong: Most Westerners have high noses.

Correct: Most Westerners have long noses.

Wrong: Are you home tomorrow.

Correct: Are you at home tomorrow.

****

Wrong: How does she look like?

Correct: What does she look like?

****

Wrong: This is the way how I did it.

Correct: This is how I did it. or This is the way I did it.

****

Wrong: How do you think about Chandigarh.

Correct: What do you think about Chandigarh.

****

Wrong: How can I do?

Correct: What can I do?

****

Wrong: "How long have you been in Mumbai?"

"Six months"

"How about Gujarati food?"

Correct: "How long have you been in Mumbai?"

"Six months"

"Do you like Gujarati food?"

****

Wrong: I visited her ill mother in the hospital.

Correct: I visited her sick mother in the hospital.

Wrong: There is a limit in my patience.

Correct: There is a limit to my patience.

****

Wrong: Please wait inside the white line.

Correct: Please wait behind the white line.

****

Wrong: Is your house insured for fire?

Correct: Is your house insured against fire?

****

Wrong: I introduce Mr. Smith to you!

Correct: May I introduce Mr. Smith to you!

****

Wrong: She was first prize.

Correct: She took first prize.

****

Wrong: Do you have any automatic camera? Yes I have it.

Correct: Do you have any automatic camera? Yes, I have one.

****

Wrong: That was a traffic accident on my way here. It is why I was late.

Correct: That was a traffic accident on my way here. That is why I was late.

****

Wrong: She is wearing blue jeans pants.

Correct: She is wearing blue jeans.

Wrong: Keep the right.

Correct: Keep to the right.

****

Wrong: Last night I didn't keep my diary.

Correct: Last night I didn't write anything in my diary.

****

Wrong: The train was late about an hour.

Correct: The train was about an hour late.

****

Wrong: He lost consciousness for a long time.

Correct: He was unconscious for a long time.

****

Wrong: He made a world record.

Correct: He set a world record.

****

Wrong: Her marriage was happy.

Correct: Her married life was happy.

****

Wrong: Maybe I think so.

Correct: I think so.

****

Wrong: The club's members are 55.

Correct: There are 55 members in the club.

****

Wrong: They didn't understand my mind.

Correct: They didn't understand what I was thinking.

Wrong: This is where you mistake.

Correct: This is where you are mistaken.

****

Wrong: I felt good mood.

Correct: I am in a good mood.

****

Wrong: Please allow me more two hours.

Correct: Please allow me two more hours.

****

Wrong: My watch doesn't move at all. I must get it checked up.

Correct: My watch isn't running, I must get it checked up.

****

Wrong: We moved house to Johor last month.

Correct: We moved to Johor last month.

****

Wrong: He is our common friend.

Correct: He is our mutual friend.

****

Wrong: It was my first time to go abroad.

Correct: It was the first time I had gone abroad.

****

Wrong: As the citizens of India, we are necessary to help the police in their fight against terrorism.

Correct: As the citizens of India, it is necessary for us to help the police in their fight against terrorism.

Wrong: I very enjoyed it.

Correct: I really enjoyed it.

****

Wrong: The children were very dangerous as the knife-wielding madman was running amok in the kindergarten.

Correct: The children were in great danger as the knife-wielding madman was running amok in the kindergarten.

****

Wrong: Mr. Trilok arrived at the office lately this morning.

Correct: Mr. Trilok arrived at the office late this morning.

****

Wrong: The sea was very rough that the ferry service had to be suspended.

Correct: The sea was so rough that the ferry service had to be suspended.

****

Wrong: It is unkind of him to ask a little child to do such many things in a day.

Correct: It is unkind of him to ask a little child to do so many things in a day.

****

Wrong: While walking along the street, I met my friend.

Correct: While walking along the street, I met a friend of mine.

****

Wrong: My this book cost me nearly 300 rupees.

Correct: This book of mine cost me nearly 300 rupees.

Wrong: Here is a pair of nice shoes.

Correct: Here is a nice pair of shoes.

****

Wrong: Is this seat empty?

Correct: Is this seat taken?

****

Wrong: Don't be noisy.

Correct: Be quiet.

****

Wrong: It is not of only your business.

Correct: It is none of your business.

****

Wrong: I will do anything I can do for you.

Correct: I will do anything I can for you.

****

Wrong: This is the key of my room.

Correct: This is the key to my room.

****

Wrong: I am going to take a two-year course of English.

Correct: I am going to take a two-year course in English.

****

Wrong: He treated me very friendly.

Correct: He treated me in a friendly way.

Wrong: This is the largest department store of the world.

Correct: This is the largest department store in the world.

****

Wrong: It's a novel of three volumes.

Correct: It's a novel in three volumes.

****

Wrong: He is a student of Harvard University.

Correct: He is a student at Harvard University.

****

Wrong: Do you know the meaning of the word of bumpy?

Correct: Do you know the meaning of the word bumpy?

****

Wrong: He had a child of his former wife.

Correct: He had a child by his former wife.

****

Wrong: She married old.

Correct: She married late in life.

****

Wrong: I saw it on the newspapers.

Correct: I read (saw) it in the newspapers.

****

Wrong: He is a liar, and you are one too.

Correct: He is a liar, and you are too.

****

Wrong: Open page 20 of your books.

Correct: Open your books to page 20.

Wrong: Our Indian students are diligent.

Correct: We Indian students are diligent.

****

Wrong: Don't make the office out of order.

Correct: Don't leave the office in a mess.

****

Wrong: My room is narrow.

Correct: My room is small.

****

Wrong: I'll visit my native place for the first time in ten years this summer.

Correct: I'll visit my birth place for the first time in ten years this summer.

****

Wrong: I was very pleasant today.

Correct: I had a very good time today.

****

Wrong: He got 87 points in chemistry.

Correct: He got an 87 in chemistry.

****

Wrong: Chang is a popular name in Taiwan.

Correct: Chang is a common name in Taiwan.

****

Wrong: I'm a public servant.

Correct: I work for the government.

Wrong: She is pure.

Correct: She is naive.

****

Wrong: I have a question to you.

Correct: I have a question to ask you.

****

Wrong: Why do you say like that.

Correct: Why do you say that?

****

Wrong: I have no house to live.

Correct: I have no house to live in.

****

Wrong: Today is hot.

Correct: It's hot today.

****

Wrong: My father will be home today afternoon.

Correct: My father will be home this afternoon.

****

Wrong: What is the total sum?

Correct: How much does it come to?

****

Wrong: We changed our train at Woodland.

Correct: We changed trains at Woodland.

****

Wrong: I travelled to Europe.

Correct: I made a trip to Europe.

Wrong: I very like swimming.

Correct: I like swimming very much.

****

Wrong: What a dirty face! Look at the mirror.

Correct: What a dirty face! Look in the mirror.

****

Wrong: The door was shut when I returned home.

Correct: The door was closed when I returned home.

****

Wrong: Wait for your turn, please.

Correct: Wait your turn, please.

****

Wrong: What time is your watch.

Correct: What time is it by your watch.

****

Wrong: I don't know what did he say.

Correct: I don't know what he said.

****

Wrong: Shall we sit in that sofa?

Correct: Shall we sit on that sofa?

****

Wrong: This steak is soft.

Correct: This steak is tender.

Wrong: His new book will be sold well.

Correct: His new book will sell well.

****

Wrong: There're a lot of sparrows stopping on the telephone lines.

Correct: There're a lot of sparrows sitting on the telephone lines.

****

Wrong: He hit me strongly.

Correct: He hit me hard.

****

Wrong: My pay cannot support my living.

Correct: My pay is not enough to live on.

****

Wrong: He wants to establish a sweet home.

Correct: He wants to establish a happy home.

****

Wrong: Why don't you take a driving license.

Correct: Why don't you get a driving license.

****

Wrong: Last year I went to Seattle. I liked there very much.

Correct: Last year I went to Seattle. I liked it very much.

****

Wrong: My mother likes to drink thick tea.

Correct: My mother likes her tea strong.

Wrong: I think it will not rain tomorrow.

Correct: I don't think it will rain tomorrow.

****

Wrong: Is your camera this kind?

Correct: Is your camera like this?

****

Wrong: His house was struck by thunder last night.

Correct: His house was struck by lightning last night.

****

Wrong: My grandmother lived to eighty-five.

Correct: My grandmother lived to be eighty-five.

****

Wrong: I have a lot of work to be done.

Correct: I have a lot of work to do.

****

Wrong: To drink too much is bad for one's health.

Correct: Drinking too much is bad for one's health.

****

Wrong: I like to paint this door to black.

Correct: I'd like to paint this door black.

****

Wrong: I have a Chinese pen friend.

Correct: I have a Chinese pen pal.

Wrong: Give me a phone.

Correct: Give me a phone call.

****

Wrong: Is there any place for me in the car?

Correct: Is there any room for me in the car?

****

Wrong: Let's play together.

Correct: Why don't you come over?

****

Wrong: My father bought me a black small leather wallet yesterday.

Correct: My father bought me a small black leather wallet yesterday.

****

Wrong: Most of the time, it is difficult for Sam in finishing his work on time.

Correct: Most of the time, it is difficult for Sam to finish his work on time.

****

Wrong: These thugs are quite capable to do really hasty things.

Correct: These thugs are quite capable of doing really hasty things.

****

Wrong: The three women quarrelled for more than an hour angrily outside the boutique.

Correct: The three women quarrelled angrily for more than an hour outside the boutique.

Wrong: You should describe what has happened detailly.

Correct: You should describe what has happened in detail.

****

Wrong: I received a letter from my sister two days before.

Correct: I received a letter from my sister two days ago.

****

Wrong: The driver, as well as four passengers, were injured in the head-on collision.

Correct: The driver, as well as four passengers, was injured in the head-on collision.

****

Wrong: The sun rises from the East.

Correct: The sun rises in the East.

****

Wrong: The thief got in from the window.

Correct: The thief got in through the window.

****

Wrong: Let's begin from page 10.

Correct: Let's begin at (on) page 10.

****

Wrong: Did you attend college?

Correct: Did you go to college?

****

Wrong: I wanted to go to Europe last summer, but it was too expensive so I gave up to go.

Correct: I wanted to go to Europe last summer, but it was too expensive so I gave up the idea.

Wrong: Leave your hand from the end of the wire.

Correct: Let go of the end of the wire.

****

Wrong: I was ten minutes late for the English lesson.

Correct: I was ten minutes late for the English class.

****

Wrong: How many Chinese letters do you know?

Correct: How many Chinese characters do you know?

****

Wrong: He is fighting for his life.

Correct: He is fighting for his bread.

****

■

Other Books on

WORD POWER SERIES

31. Self-Help to English Conversation	150/-
32. The Art of Effective Communication	125/-
33. A Book of Proverbs & Quotations	110/-
34. Word Power Made Easy	160/-
35. English Grammar Easier Way	160/-
36. General English for Competitive Examinations	160/-
37. Spoken English	125/-
38. School Essays, Letters Writing and Phrases	125/-
39. How to Write & Speak Better English	125/-
40. Quote Unquote (A Handbook of Famous Quotations)	160/-
41. Improve Your Vocabulary	150/-
42. Common Errors in English	150/-
43. The Art of Effective Letter Writing	125/-
44. Synonyms & Antonyms	125/-
45. Idioms	125/-
46. Business Letters	125/-

Lotus PRESS

Unit No. 220, 2nd Floor, 4735/22, Prakash Deep Building,
Ansari Road, Darya Ganj, New Delhi- 110002
Ph.: 32903912, 23280047, 9811594448
E-mail : lotuspress1984@gmail.com, www.lotuspress.co.in